PANTO
The MANUAL

How to put on a pantomime and make a community.

by Andrew Pastor and friends

Dedicated to the people and players of
Drimpton and surrounds.

Contents

Introduction   9

Scene Setting   11

'To do panto, or not to do panto'

ACT ONE   16

Including: Key Players. Finding the Venue. Choosing the Pantomime. Inviting the Community to join in.

ACT TWO   27

Including: The Script. Writing in Rhyme or not? Writing for Baddies. Being a Goodie – It's not for wimps! Writing Relationships.

ACT THREE   82

Including: Let's start with Costumes. Talking about Set and Scenery.

I N T E R V A L   95

Time for a breather.

ACT FOUR   96

Including: Drawing up a Rehearsal Schedule. Managing Rehearsals. How to get a performance & a few basic bits of stagecraft or 'business'. Children on stage – How to get them to give of their best (and adults, too!). Chases.

I N T E R V A L   134

Time for a another breather.

ACT FIVE   137

Including: The Last Ten Days. 'Working the Audience'. One Day To Go! – The Dress Rehearsal.

ACT SIX   **155**

Including: Business. Publicity, promotion, and getting punters through the door. Ticket Selling: 'How to get bums on seats'.

ACT SEVEN   **161**

Including: Getting Technical. Sound. Lights. Props. Production Assistants.

ACT EIGHT   **173**

Including: Extras. The Programme. Front of House. Refreshments. Bar. Making Keepsakes.

ACT NINE   **183**

Show Time!

ACT TEN   **200**

Including: Goodbye. Set, Scenery and Props. Costumes.

ACT ELEVEN   **204**

And finally ...

Appendix I - People   **213**

Appendix II - Stage Extension Pictures   **219**

Appendix III - Sound and Lighting Plot extract   **222**

Appendix IV - Rehearsal Schedule   **226**

Appendix V - List of Pantos performed   **228**

Index   **229**

PANTO: The MANUAL

with acknowledgements to:

Hilary, Lee and Mike Baker, Beryl and Ken Banks, Jenny Beck, Grace, Jenny, and Rosa Bellorini, Rod Bracher, Leigh Carroll-Smith, Emily and Sharon Chubb, Alan Clark, Dave and Rosie Crane, John and Lynwen Davies, Eleanor and Zacyntha Dunhill, Chris Fogg, Becky, Ellie, Robert and William Fooks, Alex Gibbons, Molly and Shirley Gibbs, Brian and Kate Hesketh, Anne, Ella, Joe, John and Michelle Horne, Amy, Jack, Jo and Mark House, Lottie Hyde, Danny Kirk, Bob and Diane Macleod, Norman Marsden, Charlotte and Rosie Marshall, Francis and Matthew Medley, Mel Newman, Eleanor and Kay Porteous, Alfy, Harry, Richard and Sue Rawlings, Emily, James and Melanie Russ, Bob and Rosemary Shepherd, Hans-Jürg Suter, Mary and Sam Trott

Designed by Brian Hesketh

Doodles & Cartoons by Patricia Barrett

Colour photographs from Jennie Banks, Guy Martin, Brian Hesketh, Dave Crane, Norman Marsden, Hilary Baker, Tony Gibbons and a number of unrecorded people can be viewed at *www.drimpton.org.uk*

Cover photographs:
Front - Mother Hood in 'Robin Hood'
Back - Abanana and Neuralgia in 'Aladdin and the Princesses'

'PANTO: The MANUAL' is a Village Voices publication.

© Village Voices 2015

For more on Village Voices go to *www.drimpton.org.uk*

Also by Andrew Pastor for Village Voices:

'Village Voices: Local Lives' – 2002

'Village Voices: Farming Families' – 2005

'The Nameless Stream' – 2006

'Who Were We?' - 2009

Introduction:

In 2013, at the end of the evening performance of our village panto, 'Robin Hood', I announced that it was my last one as writer/director, after having done 10 in 20 years. Then, just a few weeks later, I set out to start writing PANTO: The MANUAL. Why?

First, it seemed only right to record and celebrate the creativity of our community over two decades. And secondly, I wanted to spread the word to the wider world – to perhaps encourage other communities to do panto! After all panto brings so many people together.

You might be living somewhere which already produces homemade pantomimes. In that case feel free to compare what you do with what we have been doing all these years. Alternatively your community might just fancy the idea of having a go at panto. Maybe we can give you pointers. Who knows where panto could lead you?

While writing this book I realised that just as a panto is not made by any one individual, other voices should be heard when telling the panto story. Not just mine. So the upshot is that as you read what follows you will meet other locals who have been involved in our pantos over the years. Not just on stage. But in lots of ways. Some I interviewed. Others wrote down their memories. Many panto people, past and present, have steered my thoughts along the way.

PANTO: The MANUAL is dedicated to this chorus of contributors, whose offerings have coloured so much of what you will read. It is also dedicated to everyone else who has been involved in our panto adventure over the years. Onstage and Backstage. And it is dedicated to everyone in our audiences. We did it for ourselves, but we also did it for you. Oh, yes we did!

We have lodged colour photos to illustrate our panto experiences on our village website *www.drimpton.org.uk* . They capture much of the work and a good deal of the fun we have had over the years.

Photo: Throughout the book, wherever you see this camera icon, it tells you that a full colour picture is available on the website mentioned above. They just didn't capture the fun of panto printed in black and white.

If you have questions or would like to know more, please get in touch with me via *mail@drimpton.org.uk*.

It's time to begin ...

SCENE SETTING

'To do panto, or not to do panto'

I really hope that even if you've never been in a panto (or seen one) you know what 'panto' is, as this book isn't about to go into the history of the entertainment. It is a theatrical form unique to Britain and almost incomprehensible to people from anywhere else. I mean, have you ever tried to explain it to someone from France or Germany? Or even to a totally fluent speaker of English from Switzerland? I have such a person in mind, a friend, an anglophile who has during his career worked and lived in the UK. Even he is bemused. When I told him about our latest production, he had this to say.

> 'We would have loved to be present in the true spirit of the intrepid ethnologist-explorer, venturing into the dark heart of rural Dorset. To me for one, despite all my reading about them, many of your most time-honoured customs remain an almost alien concept...'
> [Hans-Jürg Suter]

It's not just Europeans; Americans are equally at a loss. Try as they might, they can't really get their heads around it.

Pantomime can be described briefly as 'mixing fairy tales and children's stories, with contemporary references and audience participation, making for raucous, noisy entertainment for all the family.' That is it in a nutshell, I think. As to its history, you should look elsewhere.

Even if the world at large cannot get to grips with pantomimes, the British learn all about them from a young age.

> 'The first and only Pantomime I remember going to see as a child was 'Hansel and Gretel' - I believe it was at the now defunct Weymouth Pavilion - and I was TERRIFIED! So I don't think I was ever taken to another Pantomime in my childhood!'
> [Mel Newman]

Ah, that may not be a good starting point in us selling the whole panto experience!

We have done pantos, and here we are going to tell you the 'what', the 'how' and the 'why'. Be warned: You may end up wanting to do pantos, too.

But first, who are we?

We are the village of Drimpton in west Dorset. Since 1993 we have done pantos every other year (there or thereabouts), making a total of 10 in all. We began with 'Ali Baba and the Forty Thieves' and our last was 'Robin Hood', in 2013. In between there was 'Mother Hubbard', 'Red Riding Hood' and the rest. [See Appendix V, 'Pantos Performed' for the complete list.]

Now let me make it clear, Drimpton is not the kind of place people are encouraged to relocate to on a raft of TV shows. Our village is not a chocolate box place on the tourist run. Nor are we on or near the coast – the one that is branded as Jurassic. We are tucked well away in the furthest most north-western corner of the county. We are within shouting distance of Somerset and only a handful of miles or so from Devon. We are a small place with even smaller neighbours, the hamlets of Netherhay and Greenham. Put us altogether and we are less than 200 households with a little over 400 inhabitants (probably). This lack of size should not be overlooked during the story that follows. And when we talk about Drimpton, never forget our two small neighbours; they have a significant role to play in our panto story.

So we are small and we are rural, surrounded by fields of grass with cows or sheep in. But we aren't the village we were. We have changed a great deal in the last 50 years. The old village with its unpretentious ham stone houses is still here, but these houses aren't alone. In the 1960s and again in the 2000s there were two phases of house building; the first of bungalows, the second of houses. Together they more than doubled the original housing stock. As a result the nature of our village and the people who live here has changed. A lot of villagers today are of retirement age. Of those in work most travel to the nearby towns of Chard, Yeovil, Crewkerne, Bridport or Dorchester on a daily basis. A growing number of people (if still small) work from home.

What other scene setting could be helpful? We have a church (small, mid-19th century), a chapel (small, early-19th century), a pub (thriving) and a village hall (well-used). The last of these is a central player in our story. But we don't have a school or a shop. We had these, but lost them. Our primary school was closed in the late 1960s and the last shop closed in the 1990s. This means all our children are bussed or driven by parents out of village, and all shopping means getting into a car or catching a bus or ordering online. This is typical of so many places. As a result the social life of the community is very different from what it used to be.

Before 1993 there had been shows and entertainments in the village for years - going back into the late 19th century, in fact - but no large-scale pantomimes. I confess here and now to loving panto. Why?

Panto is a great way to get together. Let's call it 'a community-building tool' if we have to. That might sound a bit worthy, but bear with me. Let me explain. Panto offers a middle ground, a neutral territory where the following happens...

- People of all ages come together in a common cause. Children learn to speak with adults outside their family and school environments. Adults learn that children are not aliens to be wary of. Breaking such barriers is priceless.

- People expand their circle of friends. Nowadays many people live semi-isolated lives. They move in limited circles and can be untrusting of others. Eyes are opened.

- People work creatively in a real-life social environment, not via some virtual social media tool.

- People make something from nothing in a short time with only the community's resources to call on. That is special.

- People are encouraged to offer and share their existing skills and talents, which are valued and recognised.

- People develop skills that can benefit the community in other ventures.

- People have FUN!

What have we to say about the community-building aspect of panto?

> 'There's a huge element in pantomime – the joining together – the team effort to do something. I didn't realise until I actually got into it. You start gently, as individuals, doing your little lines. And then you're brought in with other people – working with them. Till eventually you do the final rehearsal – where it's light-hearted and it's not too serious – and you're meeting other people and you're all working together. It was really nice for somebody who is 70-ish meeting up with, say, 7 or 8-year-olds, from the same village. That would normally not happen. And they wouldn't meet me. And you meet their parents. And parents of different children meet. And then activity outside the pantomime happens. Children become friends, which they might not have been if the panto hadn't've happened. You've got all sorts of people there. Professional people. Farming community. Retired people. Students. Everybody. You're meeting sections of village society you probably normally wouldn't come across. Even in a small village you tend to stick with your own groupings – you cross over only now and again - but this happens with the pantomime. It brings a huge part of the community together, in that one place.'
> [Danny Kirk]

I agree completely. As do others:

> 'We did it initially because we wanted to get involved in the village and have fun. It involves all ages within the community. All talents. Whether it's in the way of lines or crafts or costumes. On stage or not... It's not just when you're on stage, it spills right out into the community.'
> [Kate Hesketh]

So as I said, I liked the idea of pantos here in Drimpton. But how, back in 1992, could I be sure that villagers would be up for one? If I was going to take on the role of director, who could I recruit? After all, panto is an activity that needs people. It cannot be done alone. And this is another reason for doing it.

ACT ONE

Including: Key Players. Finding the Venue. Choosing the Pantomime. Inviting the Community to join in.

Act One – Scene One: Key Players

As with any venture, start small. Don't raise false hopes and expectations until the project becomes do-able. This was my strategy.

In order for panto to happen here, some key players needed to be sounded out; people who were able and willing to lead others; people with an appropriate track record. This was where background knowledge of the community was of paramount importance. Who had done things before? Who was an enthusiastic painter, stitcher, musician, technical whizz? These people needed to be asked, in a roundabout fashion over a cup of coffee in some cases. "If we were going to put on a village panto, would you be willing to build sets/ lead the costume making/ design scenery/ lead on the technical side/ play music?"

A creative stitcher agreed to be chief costumier. An electrician was up for doing the lighting. An artist would design backdrops and paint with her art class. A retired carpenter would happily build sets. The Chapel organist said he'd be the accompanist. We had a team. Without them Drimpton's first big panto would never have got off the ground.

Only when such key roles had ticks in their boxes did we take the next step.

Act One – Scene Two: Finding the Venue

Before going any further, make sure that you have a place where you can perform. It can be a community hall, school hall, sports hall or church hall. The key word, as I'm sure you've noticed, is 'hall'. Halls are open, utilitarian, adaptable spaces designed for public use. They are equipped with basic facilities that will help the production, eg: seating, staging and maybe lighting and a sound system. If you don't have access to such a place, then you need to think very carefully what you are going to do and how you are going to do it. And do your thinking now, before going any further. You might be adventurous spirits who fancy performing in a derelict factory, a shopping mall, a marquee or the open air. Anywhere. There are limitless possible venues. In fact, I've just thought of another one. Here goes. We all know that every town centre across the land has empty shops in ever-larger numbers. Well, I don't know if Mary Portas, 'The Queen of Shops', has thought of pumping life into our town centres by producing pop-up pantos, but I offer the idea for free. How about it? Are you up for it?

For me, putting on a panto is challenge enough. I don't want to seem to be a boring old codger, but I'd suggest you go for a traditional venue – warm, dry, safe, with working toilets!

Be absolutely certain of the venue's availability for the date(s) of the performance(s), and the major rehearsals over the last week to ten days prior. If there is a booking procedure, fill in the form and keep a copy. If you can also book the venue throughout more (or all) of the rehearsal period, so much the better. If charges are involved, go to Act Three: Scene One, Aside Ten, on pages 85-86, where I discuss finances.

So, you have your venue. In due course you are going to get to know it intimately, but at this point – before you've even decided on the panto you would like to do – you want to know the answers to the following.

- How big [=width and depth] is the acting area of the stage?
- What is the height of the acting area from stage surface to the 'ceiling'?
- How many entrances/exits does the acting area offer and where are they?
- How much off-stage space is there either side in the wings?
- Is there storage space available?

Knowing what these are might well determine your choice of panto. You can adapt many things, but you cannot change the physical dimensions of the area you are going to work in.

Act One – Scene Three: Choosing the Pantomime

Here a decision has to be made between an existing script, a completely original script written by a volunteer, or a half-way house, where, for example, non-copyright material, eg: children's nursery rhymes or fables, are used as a source. Over the years we have done all three.

Using an existing script has some advantages.

- Easily sourced from a public lending library.
- Wide choice.
- No need for you to find a writer.

There are also some disadvantages.

- Performance fees (not in all cases).
- It can be hard to find a script that is suitable for your cast/potential cast/venue and facilities.
- Often outdated material.
- Frequently depends on live music and singing. This isn't a disadvantage if your community can provide these skills.

Using an original script or adapting non-copyright material has advantages.

- Can be written with community/cast/facilities in mind.
- Limitless choice of themes.
- Flexible.
- No performance fees.

There is a major disadvantage.

- Needs time and effort and skill of a writer.

When we did our first panto we chose to do 'Ali Baba and the Forty Thieves' in a version we would adapt ourselves from 1001 Nights. Then, with a synopsis of the story worked out, we went public! Villagers were told about the concept.

Act One – Scene Four: Inviting the community to join in

> 'You caught me on a weak moment! And I couldn't come up with a good enough excuse not to. I'd never done it before, and I thought: "You've got to say you've done it at least once." '
> [Melanie Russ]

How can you get people on board? The best way is Word Of Mouth. Nothing works better. Approaching people who you know, who know you, and asking them directly is always far better than all other methods. Since 1990 we have had free village newsletters on a monthly basis delivered to every household. They work well at informing the community, but almost nobody then gets in touch with the magic words: "I've read about the panto and I want to join in!" The newsletter (or text/email) helps to prepare the ground, but I have found that everybody (bar a few) needs to be personally approached.

So that is what I do. A 'social media' tool might work well, but it is not for me. I favour real-life face-to-face. This takes time and energy, but you get tea and biscuits; something that no app delivers. And, once you've got in the house with a cup of tea, you've as good as got them!

Selling the concept – recruiting cast

The pitch needs to be adapted depending on whose door you knock on when you are recruiting cast members. For children, who are always most likely to say 'yes' quickly, they need to know that they are going to have fun. Girls are far more willing to sign up. Boys need to be sold on the idea that their characters will be loud, naughty and/or silly with lots of opportunities for falling over. This appeals to lots of girls, too. Parents need to be present when you pitch the panto so that 'commitment' can be discussed. It is far better to make it clear from the outset that before someone signs up to the panto, they realise that it is a full-scale commitment over a period of months.

The Boy Who Said 'No'

A young boy, when he was 5½ years old, was asked if he'd like to be in that year's panto. His older sister, was going to be in it, so how about him? He said 'Yes', but after just one rehearsal changed his mind. And he was not to be persuaded. But every rehearsal, when his mother brought his sister, he had to come along too. He sat out front occupied with something digital.

Wind the clock forwards two years. The lad, now aged 7½, wanted to be in that year's panto as long as he had no lines. He made that very clear. He was very happy to be one of the Dwarfs and share in everything they had to do – but no lines! Though, in reality, he was called upon to say the odd word, usually with everybody else.

Why had he changed his mind in the previous two years?

> 'Because when I saw Amy doing it I just saw myself in my head doing it. And it'd be really fun. So I said, 'Yes'.'
> [Jack House]

Recruits

> 'Every year I waited for the inevitable knock at the door of you coming to invite us to take part in the latest extravaganza.'
> [Eleanor Dunhill]

When is a child old enough to be in the cast? The youngest children to date have been four years old. My guiding principles are: Does he/she have an older sibling or parent in the cast? If so, then maybe. If not, no.

> 'She didn't want to be in the first one. At the time she was a 'shy little princess' character so she didn't really want to be up there. And then once she'd done that one, immediately she wanted more. She couldn't wait till the next one and she wanted more lines. Then she claimed she didn't have enough lines. Even though she had more.'
> [John Horne, recalling his daughter's first panto.]

> 'I thought: "Should I try this?" One half of my head said: "Yeah. Go on. Try it. It'll be fine!" The other part went: "What are you doing, James?" The first half won obviously. When I walked in there were lots of young kids. That was scary. But there were some older ones as well. The little children were crazy. But I enjoyed it. I'm glad I did it in the end.'
> [James Russ was a late starter at 14.]

Older teenage children can often respond positively to being given significant parts to play. They warm to the fact that you are showing confidence in their abilities. Girls are still more likely to say 'yes' quickly. Boys can often be persuaded into saying 'yes' if they know/think that a mate of theirs has already signed up.

Adults often respond much the same way as the children! Some really want to have Big Parts. Some definitely don't, and say, "OK, as long as I have only a few lines at most." Some only want to appear, say nothing, and exit! And the chance to be a panto cow can be irresistible!

> 'Oh, I was in the cow! With Jim. `Ee were moaning like hell all the time we was playing it, cos `ee `ad to be be`ind me. `Ee was worried I was gonna blow off. It was fun cos I did'n `ave to learn any lines. Just going "Moooo!" all the time. Great times.'
> [Mike Baker]

Women are always happiest discussing what they are going to wear.

Men are frequently worried about the whole idea of appearing on stage. They need to know that they will still be 'blokes' after the experience.

How can you get a cast reflecting the whole age range? Children and the retired will always be represented in a cast, but what about adults aged 20 to 50? These are the people with full working lives and a lot on their plates. I have discovered the only real way to recruit such people is to get their children in the cast, too. In this way everyone gains. I get help with crowd control. They get the chance to relax, have regular doses of 'foolishness', not worry what the kids are up to, and forget the serious stuff of life for a while. For many adults panto offers therapy. And that is not a joke.

> 'I had no intention of doing panto. Never had any inclination to be AmDram or anything like that. There was a Social at the Hall. You're sitting there and Andrew comes in with reams of paper. The whole Hall goes quiet. People start creeping off. You're left there. I had a cup of tea and you came up and had a chat. Then you realise you'd taken the Queen's shilling! In your tea. And you're press-ganged into it. You've got no choice. When you wake up, you're in The Panto. And I can remember everyone thinking: 'Oh he's got him' and looking at me with that sad look. That's how you get involved.'
> [Alan Clark]

> 'Andrew asked me if I would like to be in the Village Pantomime – well, how could I refuse? I am no longer able to play the pretty princess, but what I have discovered is I enjoy being evil and wicked and all the things you can do as a mature person.'
> [Mel Newman]

And even if people haven't got real stage experience they may well have other performing skills to call upon, such as the retired Navy man (no names!) who entertained a German yachting fraternity in Kiel singing rugby songs to them all night from a stage.

That is perfect preparation for performing in panto!

When you are recruiting for a pantomime you can never know what existing talents you will discover and what new ones are about to be launched.

I said above that few people volunteer, but a few do. How come? Here is the House family talking:

> Jo:
> Never ever would have dreamt of getting up on a stage. I was supposed to have been a star with lines at school, but I just stood there. Didn't say a single word.
>
> Mark:
> I did do it at school, but younger than my kids now. But if you're talking secondary school or when you become a bit more aware of yourself, no – I would've run a mile.
>
> Jo:
> But when I used to come down with Amy, doing her first one (in 2011), going to all the rehearsals, seeing everybody enjoying themselves, I thought: "I wanna be part of that."
>
> Mark:
> It does everybody a lot of good. At the Christmas Show (in 2012) you announced the panto and it was the first time we knew it. Us and the Rawlings we just went up and put our names down. We didn't know what we were gonna do.
>
> Jo:
> Not until you met Sue Rawlings and me up at the bus stop. And you said to us, "Would you like lines?" And I said, "Just a few."
>
> Mark:
> I had seen you round the block and there was a hint as to what I might be up to. So I think I knew when I signed the type of character I might do. And it did us all the world of good.
>
> Jack:
> And I had fun, too.
>
> Amy:
> Fun for all the family.
>
> Jo:
> Amy started it.
>
> Jack:
> Thank you, Amy!

Of course, there are some people who will make it very clear that appearing on stage isn't for them. And unlike Jack they aren't about to change their minds. People like them make up the panto's audience. They play a very important role. Without them why do we do it?

Before you leave your potential recruits you talk about 'availability'. In fact you might talk about that almost at the very start of your pitch. "Hello, I'm here to see if you'd like to be in our village panto. But before going any further let's talk about dates. It is on Saturday March 28th. Can you check that you've not got any special event planned for that day..." They check. Nothing in the diary, so you can continue your pitch. You really don't want to spend time selling the project only to find after half-an-hour that they have a family wedding on March 28th. Also at this very early stage you need to know if there are any other periods when they already know they won't be available – say, a three week holiday in Trinidad in February. Lucky them. This greatly affects how you cast them. If you are going to do 'Aladdin' and you discover the person you had half-hoped would play the evil Vizier is going to be on that cruise in the West Indies, you have a decision to make. Giving him the role would make scheduling rehearsals very difficult and make it hard for the other performers in scenes with him as acting with an imaginary person, to a space, is never a good thing. He could, of course, still be in the panto, but in a smaller role.

The purpose of this recruitment drive is to get the word out and drum up numbers. I usually don't tell people what specific parts they will play. It's all left vague. Just getting them to say they'll be in it is the aim.

ACT TWO

Including: The Script. Writing in Rhyme or not? Writing for Baddies. Being a Goodie – It's not for wimps! Writing Relationships.

Act Two – Scene One: The Script

So now you have a pool of talent to cast from. Though there will be more who want to join in once the thing becomes a fact, you know roughly the numbers you are working with, and so you can write/adapt/tinker with your script. By the way, the tinkering goes on throughout the entire panto period. But if you are working with a professional script, there is not so much room for manoeuvre, not without infringing copyright. Having said that, such scripts are often written with an eye to changing numbers, - a flexible number of townspeople at the fair, or the potential for whole herds of woodland animals. But these characters will never get themselves more than 'group lines', shouting 'Oh, yes, you did!', cheering the goodies, booing the baddies. This is, however, all necessary stuff in a panto, and many cast members want nothing more.

If you are writing/adapting your script, here are my rules of thumb.

- Every character must have a name. Nobody is simply 'a child' or 'another child'. [For more on this, see *Aside One – Naming*, which is coming shortly, on page 31.]

- Every character has at least one line on his/her own. This might only appear late on in the rehearsal period when confidence has grown.

- Characters have scenes in recognisable groups. If we take 'Robin Hood' as an example. There were Robin Hood and His Merry Men and Maids (5 teenagers), Snow White and the

Dwarfs (15 people, including all the under-11s), Big Bad Wolf and Three Little Pigs (4 people), Sheriff, Lady and Guards (6 people), Lumberjacks (4 people), Mother Hood and Market Traders (7 people). It makes for team building and ease of rehearsing which needs to be borne in mind, even at this early stage.

- Whatever your storyline is, there must be the possibility for expansion or contraction. You have Pirates, Fairies, or Soldiers, etc, but no specific number. In this way you can accommodate later recruits or handle shortages.

- Whatever characters your youngest performers are playing, they will need a grown-up leader to work with. This is an adult or older teenager who likes children and that the children will like in return. So, for example, they are Soldiers for the Grand Old Duke of York, Pirates for the Pirate Captain, Gnomes for the Evil Witch, Fairies for the Fairy Headmistress, Thieves for Abanellie, the Queen of Thieves, or Mother Hubbard's children.

- Do you have a 'Dame' or not? Audiences respond well to them. Traditionally a Dame is played by a man. But we have frequently had Dames played by feisty women with a sense of fun!

- What about a Principal Boy? This is when the young male hero is played by a girl/woman. The character is a Goodie and not funny. This is a hard role to perform well. We have avoided the problem by not having them.

- Front of Curtain Scenes. If your venue has stage curtains that can open and close, Front of Curtain Scenes help you change sets/scenes unseen and keeps the action flowing. There is nothing worse than long periods when an audience sits in the dark waiting for the next scene to start.

- Not too many sets. Of course this depends on your set-building and scenery-making teams, but the less set changes the easier it is. A few beautiful, clever, interesting sets are better than lots of less well-made ones. Every set change takes time.

- As you are writing/adapting the script, bear in mind the practicalities of the venue. Every venue has its limitations – size of performance area, size of offstage area, number of potential entrances and exits, etc, as we have discussed above. If you can, take the significant limitations into account.

- An Interval is obligatory! Time for toilet visits, taking tea and maybe visiting a bar. Time to stretch legs and natter. Chairs in amateur venues are often uncomfortable after an hour. The interval is a good time for your major set change. Bear this in mind when the script is being written or chosen.

- Script length should be no more than 2¼ hours max running time. An A4 page of ordinary text, eg: Arial font size 10, usually takes about 4 minutes to perform. Of course, if the page has 'business' in it – eg: a chase - it will take longer, maybe much longer. Again taking 'Robin Hood' as an example. The show had 28 pages and ran for 2¼ hours, making it over 4¾ minutes per page.

- Audience participation. If audiences expect one thing from your panto, it is the chance to shout 'Behind you!', 'Oh, yes, he did!' (and all its variants), and to boo and cheer at regular intervals. This must be catered for.

- Characters spend as much time talking directly to the audience as they do to each other.

- Bad jokes. Everyone likes a good bad joke, something to groan at. If you aren't a natural teller of such jokes, there are lots of joke books in print, which cover every topic under the sun. And you could ask the children in your community, as they know a store of jokes, some old and others topically up-to-date.

- Your Goodies must be lovable. Give them the chance to engage with the audience. Eg: "Hello, I'm Snow White. Pleased to meet you. All of you. [no response?] I said hello. [response] That's better. I know we are going to be friends…"

- Your Baddies must be Bad, but not harshly offensive. Insulting the audience is a fine line that must be walked by Baddies. "OK you rural rabble, you dimwitted Drimptonians, stop sucking your thumbs and listen!…"

- Your Baddies must have 'The Plan' by which they are going to get what they are after.

- Local and topical references are a plus, especially in negative comments by the Baddies. Members of the audience from neighbouring villages/communities/towns expect it!

- References to highly popular TV programmes, the latest blockbuster film and their stars work well, as do well-known catchphrases. 'I don't believe it!' Hence the Lumberjacks in 'Robin Hood' believe they sing so well that they should appear in the next series of The Axe Factor (geddit?).

- Slapstick. There must be mess, chaos, noise, fallings over. Eg: a cookery scene that prepares horrible food which unsuspecting characters eat; a laundry scene where the mangle begins to swallow characters; a decorator's scene that includes the foot-in-bucket, wallpaper-paste-in-the-face, and foot-through-wallpaper-up-a-ladder jokes. These take more rehearsing than scenes with lines.

- Chases! In a typical venue such as a village or school hall, chases through and round the audience are a must and need to be considered when writing.

- There must be a convincing resolution in which the Goodies beat the Baddies and everyone lives happily ever after.

'I remember when Andrew decided to write the first panto, he went round to all the children living in the village and asked them to collect favourite jokes, then post them through his front door. He then proceeded to incorporate all of these jokes into the script. Brilliant. So instead of trying to adapt existing scripts to fit the village, Andrew instead always wrote original, bespoke scripts, taking such care to tailor them to meet the needs of whoever had volunteered to be in it, so that there was a part specially created for each individual. Wonderful!'
[Chris Fogg]

Thank you. But too much praise could go to my head!

Aside One – Naming

As I said above, all characters must have a name. Why do I feel that so strongly?

Let us think about the moment when parts are allocated to the cast. The Director tells someone they are going to be a Guard, or, he/she tells them they are going to be Erbert, who is a guard. The message, I feel, is a very different one. The name immediately gives the person playing him a mental picture. He has an identity. This means that he can tell others who he is. He's not just 'one of the guards'; he's Erbert. As such he is on equal footing with every other member of the cast, because everyone has a named part.

There is another reason, too. When writing dialogue, if characters have no names, the pronouns 'you', 'he', 'him', 'she', 'her', 'them' have to be used all the time. As a result the relationships are never as personal as they are when names are used. Nor does the dialogue sound as interesting.

And finally, if every character has a name, it allows a 'register' scene when characters are introduced to the audience. They can do this themselves; the Dwarfs are made to do it by Snow White in 'Robin Hood' to get over their shyness. Or a roll call can be taken by another character as happens when Charlie Chizzlewick, as Commander-in Chief, reviews the soldiers in 'The Grand Old Duke of York'.

If you are writing your own material, naming characters is, I find, great fun. Names say so much about what your characters are like. Indulge your imagination to the full.

Traditional panto characters come to you already named, but don't let that stop you. What was Mother Hubbard called at birth? She certainly wasn't called 'Mother', was she? So why not call her Aubergine, as we did. Then, when we did 'Red Riding Hood', Red's Grandmother, who we all know lives in a cottage in the wood, could not remain nameless. We christened her Dame Desdemona Trot. Panto gives you license to call anyone anything.

Coming are examples from some of our pantos:

In our version of Aladdin there were no less than eight Princesses. Why? Well we had eight girls wanting to be princesses, so it was the right thing to do. They were duly named Li-Lo, Shang-Hi, Foo-Yong, Feng-Shui, Ming-Varz, Sat-Suma and Sing-Song.

The other girls and boys fancied being pirates in the same panto, and they were Cutthroat, Scarface, Pimple, Piggy, Snotnose, Badbreath, and Nigel, who was the intellectual one of the outfit. I hope you are beginning to get the picture.

In 'The Magic Cupboard' we met the staff and pupils of Mrs Fenella Figtree's School for Fairyfolk. Mrs Figtree was the Dame, in the mould of the late, great Alistair Sim in the original St Trinian's. The pupils were Millicent Feathersoft, Ariadne Candlelight, Vesper Gloaming, Tristana Moonbeam, Phoebe Thistledown, Delilah Night-Moth, Felicity Glimmer, Zazu Appleblossom. Lulu-Belle Lullaby, Gloria Starshine and Clarissa Snowflake. All very pretty as I'm sure you'll agree. That's not to say the characters weren't above getting into mischief, because they were.

In 'Dick Whittington' we met rats in number. They were Scratchit, Sniffit, Basher, Toothless, Twitcher, Gnasher, Scrabbler, Nibbler, Sneezer, Dribbler and Squeak. All are members of the gang led by Julius Cheeser and his partner, Cleo-ratra. None of them could be called nice, but all of them enjoyed their nastiness a great deal.

Pantos have Kings and Queens. They have courts full of courtiers and kitchens full of staff. Everyone needs a name. Among the royalty we meet at various times are Ermintrude, Queen of Hearts, Emperor Foo Wiff Pong and King Pippin the Peerless. At their courts they are served by Sir Nautilus Necktie, Lord Bonio Winalittle and Nurse Nasturtium. While in their kitchens Martha Panwipe, Ada Taradiddle and Clara Cheeseparcel are doing as little as they can safely get away with.

Photo: King Pippin and Queen Peardrop - costumes and set made by villagers.

And finally, we come to the major Baddies. Now you need to distil the essence of their badness and condense it in their names. We have boo-ed Frostina Fireblight, who was a very wicked witch, with her ghoul of a partner, Mildew. We have spent time in the unpleasant company of Speculum, Sheriff of Nottingham, and his gold-digging wife, Lady Wilhelmina Thigh-Slapper, and the equally horrible Norbert Slopbucket, the Knave of Hearts, and his paramour, Septicaemia. When it comes to the naming of Baddies, be as gruesome and unpleasant as you like.

And if you really can't think of names, look around you. Take a word, any word. 'Mug' for example. Now Marmaduke Mug sounds like a dim, titled aristocrat, and Marmaduke Mug-Lightly, sounds dimmer. Martha Mug, works in the castle kitchen and if she is Scottish, she's Martha McMug. Take another word – 'Spatula'. It sounds feminine to me. Spatula could be a goodie or a baddie - a horrible spook or the daughter of King ... King... King Pepperpot and Queen Paprika! Like I say, pick words out of the blue and play with them. Often true panto names appear.

33

Act Two – Scene Two: Writing in Rhyme, or not?

Sometimes we've rhymed, and sometimes we've not.
It decides on the characters and on the plot.
Baddies can do it to present their foul schemes.
Witches might tell us their evillest dreams.
Fairies can rhyme for the granting of wishes,
But then the only words you can find for a real rhyme are 'fishes'...or 'dishes'.

Yes, writing rhyme has its problems.

Writing a complete panto in rhyme is not for me. But here's a scene from 'Aladdin and The Princesses' where the trio of Baddies - Abanazar, the Magician, Abanana, his wife, and their horrible daughter, Neuralgia (medical conditions are a good source for the naming of baddies), move into rhyme as they address the Audience.

Abanazar:
  Abanazar is my name.
  Absolute power is my game.
Abanana:
  He has brought you here to watch him win
  Complete control of old Peking.
Abanazar:
  Don't be deceived. I hate you all.
  You'll watch me rise; I'll see you fall.
Neuralgia:
  It's boys and girls he most despises
  For picking noses and telling lies-es.
Abanana:
  Little ones he likes, of course:
  Grilled on toast with lots of sauce!

Abanazar:
   Now to the plot: I have a scheme
   Following a recent magic dream.
   I clearly saw – it was foretold,
   The world in my wicked stranglehold!
   The Emperor here has eight young daughters.
Neuralgia:
   Each one of which I'd gladly slaughter!
Abanazar:
   I plan to make them disappear,
   And replace them all with Neuralgia here.
Neuralgia:
   Oh, Daddy Dearest, darling ducky.
   I never knew I'd be so lucky.
   But I am the prettiest, and with such a face
   It's only fair I rule the place.
[Abanazar and Abanana cough meaningfully.]
Abanana:
   With us both to guide you, and lead the way,
   Our family will make the Emperor pay.
Abanazar:
   It's early morning; the sun is breaking,
   And time for us to go trouble-making. Hah, hah!
[They exit.]

In this panto the Baddies rhyme between themselves or when Abanazar employs his magical powers. All three of them step out of rhyme when talking to other characters, or with asides, or to insult the audience! All of the other characters speak 'normally' all of the time.

📷 Photo: Abanana, Abanazar and Neuralgia.

As the utterly horrible Neuralgia, Zacyntha Dunhill, then aged 15, had her life-changing chance to be BAD! It was 2000. [See Back Cover photograph.] Here is her account:

'A person's life can be made up of many momentous events; such occasions can make or shape us into the people we are today. For some, such examples may include travelling alone to a foreign country, kissing a dearly loved one Goodbye, looking into the eyes of a new-born baby.

For me, defining moments have included being awarded my first ever 'A', getting a set of Curling Tongs for Christmas, leaving home for the first time, and of course, that all important realisation that being a 'Goth' may not actually suit me.

But, there is one moment, which trumps all of these given examples; one moment where I can say with absolute certainty, "Yes, I had 'made it'. Yes, I had finally 'arrived'." And that was the moment when I was delivered the news that I had the lead role in our Village Pantomime!

Oh, the years I had spent braving the harsh winter cold, walking the uphill route to rehearsals, knowing that every time I left the house I was risking my life (there was no pavement). I had spent years working my way up the local community's Am-Dram ladder, striving to prove myself, waiting patiently in the wings. The time had finally come for me to evolve, now was my time to shine!

The pantomime was to be 'Aladdin and the Princesses' and the best news I received yet was that my character was to be a BADDIE!!!

Oh, how I threw myself into character ('Method Acting' being my preferred technique), stropping whenever I could - well, I did this all the time anyway - only this time, I actually had an excuse - my character was a Baddie! It was as though my whole life had been leading up to this moment. All those personality flaws I carried could finally be put to good use.

Even though the pantomime was (obviously) light-hearted, I took my role very seriously - I booked a computer at Crewkerne Library so I could internet search "Evil Leaders". I conferred with my Costume Designer (Mum) over suitable outfits. Hell, I even highlighted my lines on the script!

I had the best time ever during rehearsals. David Crane and Hilary played my Parents, and I remember me and

Hilary had to 'out-baddie' each other (purely as characters you see - our on-stage rivalry did not seep into the local community).

The day of our first show I felt a feeling of absolute fear and dread, but I needn't have worried. The audience loved me, and I in turn hated them. Well, I was a Baddie after all!

But in all seriousness, I loved the attention. Me and Hilary really played up to the audience and lapped up all the 'Boos' and 'Hisses' our characters brought.'

Photo: Abanana and Neuralgia.

Rhyming also works well in extended chants. The junior rats, a.k.a. 'The Ratlings', in 'Dick Whittington', resort to rhyme to get their message across.

> Ratlings:
> We are The Ratlings, cool and mean.
> We've got more street cred than you've ever seen.
> We're baddest of the bad. We're never ever good.
> The roughest, toughest rodents in the whole neighbourhood!
>
> We are The Ratlings, sharp as ice.
> No one ever loves us cos we're naughty, not nice.
> We're coolest of the cool. We make you look like fools.
> The ratty tatty army are the ones that rule!

Children in a cast enjoy this sort of thing and do it with lots of enthusiasm.

The only characters, who operate a great deal in rhyme, are the 'magicals' – the Witches who curse and blight what they touch, and the Fairy Godmothers who step in with spells to win the day.

Here is an example of witches in full flow. It is from 'The Grand Old Duke of York'. Baron Grabbit is about to make a pact with the formidable trio of Ammonia Ashtray, Frostia Fungus and Trivia Trash.

Baron:
> I'm going to chop down Charlie before he can get in my way. I'm the boss around here and don't let anyone forget it. You may call me hard-hearted, cold blooded and wicked to the core. I just say, 'How right you are!'
> The time has definitely come to dump the dim Duke!

[The three Witches return suddenly and unannounced. Baron drops to his knees in fear.]

Ammonia:
> Ah, Baron Grabbit, is it not?

Frostia:
> Your heart as cold as ice
> Hugs to itself an evil plot.

Trivia:
> Such a nasty dream. Not nice.

[The Witches cackle.]

Baron:
> *[unnerved]* How do you know?

Ammonia:
> Oh, Grabbit, when wickedness is brewing
> We taste it on the air.

Frostia:
> We hear it ticking in your heart.

Trivia:
> We know the secrets you don't share.

Ammonia:
> If you so wish, we'll lend our skills to make your dream come true.

All Witches:
> The Grand Old Duke shall be destroyed, and York belong to you!

Baron:
> Oh, yes! Yes! Anything you say!

All Witches:
> Promise!

Baron:
> Cross my heart and hope to...*[He stops himself. Witches cackle.]*

All Witches:
> *[casting their spell]* Hocus pocus. Riddle-me-ree.
> Our spell is cast. Fie. Foe. And fee.

> Ammonia:
> [hands over scroll] Here is our plan.
> Trivia:
> In the deep dark woods at the midnight hour.
> Frostia:
> Do not be late. You'll receive the power.
> Trivia:
> For you, the Baddie, the future will be good.
> Ammonia:
> The goodie Duke will lose it all
> All Witches:
> At midnight... in the wood.
> [They exit cackling.]
> Baron:
> [scans plan] With the wicked witches on my side nothing can go wrong...

[That's what the Baron thinks. But he is mistaken!]

Photo: The Witch, Rosa Mouldyteeth.

And having met Abanazar, Baron Grabbit, and other Baddies above it's time to talk about...

Act Two – Scene Three: Writing for Baddies

> 'The Baddie's much more fun than anything else. It's much better playing the Baddie than the Goodie. You can milk it and you get all the audience's reactions.'
> [Beryl Banks]

I have said earlier that Baddies must be Bad. I feel there is a 'Baddie style' of writing.

A useful tool is alliteration. This sounds a bit complicated (or even painful) but in fact it just means putting together strings of words that have the same initial sounds. Add to that an old-style, elaborate vocabulary and the result can make for a Baddie the audience wants to boo.

It is ideal for insulting the local Audience:

> ...namby pamby Netherhay nincompoop nobodies!
> ...grubby gang of gormless Greenham goonies!
> ...dismal dimwitted Drimpton do-nothings!

If this doesn't get the Audience boo-ing, nothing will, especially as the character giving out the insults is being acted by someone they know very well in real life! It has to be said that all Baddies (and the people playing them) enjoy the insults and deliver them with great relish. (innocently: I cannot think why.) It is often in this area where the most inspired adlibbing takes place.

Baddies have fun, not being themselves for a while.

> 'I have really enjoyed being the Baddie. Partly because with the make-up and wigs and things. In 'The Magic Cupboard' when I was The Knave of Hearts I had a very nice black wig and full make-up on and somewhere in the second half of the panto a voice in the audience suddenly said: "Oh my God, that's my doctor!" They'd watched the whole of the first half and only then realised who I was.'
> [John Horne]

Alliteration for the fun of alliterating

Sometimes other characters can indulge in such verbal fun and games, as in a scene from 'Mother Hubbard'. The characters include Jack Horner, Contrary Mary, Tweedledum, Tweedledee, Simple Simon, Margery Daw, five Police Constables and Tom Piper's sister, Petra, who is a pepper seller.

> *Petra:*
>   *[entering] Pickled Pepper! Pickled Pepper. A penny a pinch for Petra Piper's Pickled Pepper!*
> *Jack:*
>   *Hello, Petra. Seen Tom?*

Petra:
> [suggestively] Playing pat-a-cake with the Princess, perhaps!

Mary:
> [surprised] Your brother, Tom, and Princess Marigold?

Petra:
> Possibly.

Mary:
> I smell trouble.

Simon:
> [checking his shoe] Well, it's not me.

Mary:
> Take one princess and one poor lad. Put them together and the result is always the same.

T.Dum:
> Bother.

T.Dee:
> Pother.

Margery:
> And fuss.

Petra:
> Probably...[resumes selling] Pickled Pepper!. Pickled Pepper! A penny a...WHAT? [She quickly checks the number of packets on her tray.] WHAT?!...[checks them again] I've been pilfered and purloined! Police! Police!

[Sounds of whistles as Constables Stoppem, Nabbem, Grabbem, Nickem, and Bookem enter.]

All Cons:
> Hello, hello, hello, hello, hello.

Stoppem:
> What's all this then?

Petra:
> Someone's pinched a peck of my pickled pepper.

Nabbem:
> A peck of pickled pepper has been pinched?

Petra:
> Precisely.

Grabbem:
> But who would want to pinch a peck of pickled pepper?

Nickem:
> There's not much precedent for the pinching of pecks of pepper, pickled or otherwise.

Petra:
> My pickled pepper's popular with plenty of people.

Bookem:
> Plenty of people are partial to your pickled pepper?

Petra:
> The public are particularly partial.

Stoppem:
> Where did you last purvey a peck of your particularly popular pickled pepper?

Petra:
> At Parson Peter Pearson's Parsonage.

Nabbem/Grabbem/Nickem/Bookem:
> At Parson Peter Pearson's Parsonage – aha!

Petra:
> Yes, I popped in for a piece of Parson Pearson's pease pudding. I parked my pickled pepper on the parsonage path and some pilfering pickpocketing pirate pinched it!

T.Dum:
> [as Constables are all busy writing] How was it packed?

Petra:
> In pepper pots.

T.Dee:
> [confirming] In pots for pepper?

Petra:
> And then in paper packets.

T.Dum:
> [confirming] And then in packets...

T.Dee:
> Made of paper.

T.Dum & T.Dee:
> [producing them from their pockets] Like these?

Stoppem:
> It's the pair of pickled pepper pinchers!

Nabbem/Grabbem/Nickem/Bookem:
> Prepare for prison!

Nabbem:
> A deep

Grabbem:
> *Dark*

Nickem:
> *Depressing*

Bookem:
> *Dungeon*

Stoppem:
> *With a lifelong lock.*

T.Dum & T.Dee:
> *[shouting] Excuse us!! [silence] Thank you.*

T.Dee:
> *We...*

T.Dum:
> *That is him.*

T.Dee:
> *And me.*

T.Dum:
> *Us, in fact.*

T.Dee & T.Dum:
> *[to each other] Exactly.*

T.Dum:
> *Well, we were walking.*

T.Dee:
> *Or strolling.*

T.Dum:
> *But not skipping.*

T.Dee:
> *Or hopping.*

T.Dum:
> *Or prancing.*

T.Dee:
> *When we found the pickled pepper outside...[pause]*

T.Dum & T.Dee:
> *Paddy's Pantry!*

Petra:
> *[embarrassed] P...P...P...*

T.Dee:
> *Paddy's*

T.Dum:
> *Pantry.*

[Constables put away their notebooks.]

Stoppem:
   So the peck of pickled pepper,
Nabbem:
   Produced by Petra Piper,
Grabbem:
   Was never actually pinched.
Nickem:
   But placed outside the portal,
Bookem:
   [knowingly] Of a presentable pastry chef whose products are particularly popular with Petra.
All Constables:
   A-ha!
All [except Petra]:
   Precisely!... A-ha!

Act Two – Scene Four: Being a Goodie – It's not for wimps!

Goodies are not wet or wimpish! They enjoy light-hearted fun and have sunny dispositions, but never think for a moment that they can't be feisty. Individually they might not stand much of a chance against the Baddies, but put them together and they become a fighting force, which can be frightening to behold (if you are a Baddie, that is). Co-operation and community spirit are their strengths. Even the prettiest Princess who dresses in pink is made of sterner stuff. Here we meet Princess Marigold, the loving daughter of the royal family in 'The Magic Cupboard', showing steely determination. Christopher Crotchet, the palace servant, who is trying to keep the Princess on the boringly straight and narrow, is having a hard time.

Christopher:
  Hold it right there, Princess!
Princess:
  You can't talk to me like that!
Christopher:
  I was given strict instructions by your father, His Majesty Old King Cole. Instructions of the strictest strictness. Instructions so strict that strict isn't the word for their strictness. Never before have there been such strict instructions in the world of Nursery Rhyme Land. In fact...
Princess:
  [interrupting] Yes, Christopher, I get the message.
Christopher:
  They are non-negotiable, unequivocal and indisputable.
Princess:
  [aside to audience] Which are all long words that mean 'strict'.
Christopher:
  As a result I have told you precisely 755 times that you can't...
Princess:
  [interrupting] Can't? Can't? Look, I will NOT be escorted everywhere I go, no matter what my father says. I am going to go out alone.
Christopher:
  You don't mean?
Princess:
  Solo.
Christopher:
  You can't be saying?
Princess:
  By myself.
Christopher:
  What are you suggesting?
Princess:
  Without anyone else.
Christopher:
  Maybe you have misunderstood your father's wishes.
Princess:
  Without you!

Christopher:
   [shocked] No!
Princess:
   And that's that!
Christopher:
   But your highness, it's late. It is in fact very late.
Princess:
   Nonsense.
Christopher:
   It's past midnight.
Princess:
   So?
Christopher:
   It's more than my job's worth. [paying for sympathy] And that's no more than a tin of beans at today's prices. You have no idea what it is like to have your credit crunched on a daily basis.
Princess:
   [more kindly] Oh, I'm not blaming you, Christopher.
Christopher:
   You've never known what it is like to have your shares shaved, your stocks shafted, your gilts go rusty and your pounds plummet.
Princess:
   I know you're only doing what my father tells you – but I'm not a child. I know what's what.
Christopher:
   You do? [Princess nods.] Oh, dear.
Princess:
   Besides what harm can come to me in Nursery Rhyme Land?
Christopher:
   If I lose sight of you for even a second, his majesty will tear up my testimonials.
Princess:
   No, he won't.
Christopher:
   He'll rubbish my references.
Princess:
   No, he won't.

Christopher:
>He'll crush my credentials.

Princess:
>No, he won't! Because his majesty will not know unless someone tells him. And you wouldn't do that, would you? [to Audience] And you wouldn't do that either, would you? [Audience: 'No'] I can't stay all day everyday in that stuffy old palace. I must get out. Spread my wings. Do a thousand things I've never done before!

Christopher:
>[aside to Audience] Sounds like she's got a song coming on.

Princess:
>The only men I ever meet are old and boring. Oh, whatever happened to all those handsome dashing knights on white horses? With shining armour, helmets and knowing smiles?...

… [unfortunately the horrible Knave of Hearts has heard all this and Princess Marigold is about to become the focus of his unwanted and worrying attention.]

Act Two – Scene Five: Writing Relationships

Panto is full of relationships - romantic, or quasi-romantic, mutually dependent or competitive. The Dame and her Beau. The Hero and Heroine. The Hero/Heroine and his/her Team of Goodies. The Villain/Villainess and his/her Other Half. The Villain/Villainess and his/her Cronies.

"There is nothing like a Dame…"

But what kind of Dame is in your panto? You need to have that clear before she is given lines to say. In no particular order here are some possible types.

- Les Dawson's 'Ada' – old-style working class woman, with curlers and apron, loose dentures and arms folded tightly underneath her chest.

- Paul O'Grady's 'Lily Savage' – tarty, caustic, brazenly glamorous, hard as a nut.

- Barry Humphries's 'Dame Edna Everage' – sharp, working class but with aspirations to being middleclass if not better, glamorous in a Queen Motherly way.

- Danny La Rue – the female impersonator, aspiring to be more feminine than almost any real woman, scarily convincing, never less than ultra glamorous.

- David Walliams and Matt Lucas's 'Emily and Florence' – very much 'Ladies' even if they do have moustaches.

- Women as portrayed by any of the Monty Python team – all of them loud and falsetto.

The list is as long as you like to make it. The question is: 'Which kind of Dame is yours going to be?' Once the writer knows, he/she can proceed to write for her.

But you can never predict how an audience will respond.

> 'When Brian came on as the Fairy Headmistress, Fenella Figtree, a little kid started crying! So funny!'
> [Ella Horne]

The Dame & her Beau – a rambunctious relationship

Clearly she is besotted with him. Clearly he is incompetent, a wimp, not worthy enough. She is (in her own eyes) a thing of beauty, taste and class with better dress sense than any topflight model. She is, in short, irresistible; yet he resists (until the very end, that is). She dotes; he tries to do a runner. And the language they use?

Here is a scene from 'The Magic Cupboard'. Mother Hubbard has targeted Georgie Porgie.

Photo: Georgie Porgie and Mother Hubbard.

Georgie:
[entering, addresses Audience] Well, hello. I'm Georgie Porgie. Heard of me? Well, have you? You're right. I'm the lad who kissed the girls and made them cry. But that was long ago. Longer ago than I want to remember. [Mother Hubbard enters unseen by Georgie.] Mind you, I'm still known as the local Don Juan. It's just that nowadays the prettiest girls Don Juan anything to do with me. Geddit? I only attract the old battleaxes. One of the oldest is Mother Hubbard. Have you met her? You have. Goodness knows how old she is. How

old do you think? *[Georgie gets different ages from the Audience and picks the oldest or suggests a higher figure.]* It's hard to tell because she's had her face lifted so many times. Now she's only got to raise her eyebrows and her socks go up. Here, shall I tell you something else? She's been trying to get me to propose to her for more than ten years, but I've always been too...*[At last he sees her.]* too... too poor to ask you to marry me. But now...NOW... it's going to be different.

Mother H:
Yes, because you're going to be too dead to ask me!

Georgie:
Aubergine, sweetheart – listen. I'm going to get myself a job. Honest, I am.

Mother H:
[scornfully] Get yourself a job! Get yourself a job! That's a laugh. You're so lazy, if you had the seven-year-itch, you'd be six years behind with your scratching. Look at you. You swallowed a teaspoon 25 years ago and you haven't stirred since.

Georgie:
Be fair. Given the chance I could be a really steady worker.

Mother H:
Steady!? If you were any steadier, you'd be stock still.*[mellowing]* Look, Georgie, I know it's hard finding work these days. It says in the papers there's thousands of jobs in jeopardy.

Georgie:
That's all right then. I'll go to jeopardy. I don't mind travelling. Not when it means we can settle down. Together at last.

Mother H:
Huh! It's no use trying to pull the wool over my thighs.

Georgie:
But it's true. Aubergine, you are one of those rare women with everything a red-blooded man could wish for.

Mother H:
[flattered] Oooh! And what exactly is that?

>   Georgie:
>   >   Bulging muscles. Legs like tree trunks. And a spare set of false teeth.
>   Mother H:
>   >   [exploding] What! [She attacks. He ducks.] Stand still and be killed!
>   [Georgie exits chased by Mother Hubbard.]...

Aside Two – Dames – Competitors for affection

In some pantos we have had pairs of Dames (or Dame-type characters). They are born to bicker and outdo each other. One such pair of competitive Dames are Ladies Clothilde Crabapple and Sylvestra Sourgrapes, who introduce themselves in the section entitled 'Double Acts' on pages 70-74. Another pair appear in 'Dick Whittington'. Peggoty and Polyanthus Chinwag are Alderman Fitzwarren's cook and housekeeper, who are never happier than when they are teasing and taunting each other. Fast forward to Act Five: Scene One, pages 139-141, where the topic is 'Working the Audience', if you want to meet them now.

The Hero and Heroine – first love

This is the understated, tongue-tied approach to relationship-building as is to be seen in this first meeting of Dick Whittington and Alice Fitzwarren, who incidentally were being played by two 14-year-olds. Puss-in-Boots (who for the sake of our panto was playing the role of Dick Whittington's far-from-silent Cat) is also present...

>   [Dick is sweeping Alderman Fitzwarren's shop.]
>   Puss:
>   >   [seeing Alice enter, aside to Audience] Ah, and who's this?
>   Alice:
>   >   [entering, aside to Audience] Who's this boy?
>   Dick:
>   >   [noticing Alice, aside to Audience] Who's that girl?
>   Alice:
>   >   [to Puss, tickling her under her chin] And who's this

pretty little kitty? [Puss is not pleased.] Kutchy-kutchy-koo! [to Dick] Is she with you?
[Puss embarks in a long mimed explanation of her own 'story so far' with plenty of mewing.]

Alice:
Do you think she's all right?
[Puss 'repeats' her story.]

Dick:
[ignoring Puss] Allow me to introduce myself. I'm Dick Whittington.

Alice:
And I'm Alice Fitzwarren. My father's a shopkeeper. [PAUSE] He owns a shop. [PAUSE] In fact he owns this shop. [PAUSE] The shop in which you are sweeping. [PAUSE] Why are you sweeping?

Dick:
Me? Sweeping? [notices broom] So I am. [PAUSE] With this broom. [PAUSE] I'm just helping Jack. [PAUSE] He's not very well.

Alice:
[sceptical] Really! Look, Jack's such a lazy lad, he tried to get a job at the baker's last year because he thought it'd be one long loaf...[PAUSE to see if Dick will get the joke]...and he thought he'd make a lot of dough. [PAUSE, Dick at last gets the joke. He laughs. They both laugh. Another PAUSE.]

Dick:
[putting broom down] Well, that's that done. [LONG PAUSE] I suppose I'd best be going.

Puss:
[aside to Audience, shocked] What?

Alice:
I suppose I should be getting along, too.

Puss:
[aside to Audience, more shocked] What??

Dick:
Tell Jack where I've left the...er...

Alice:
The broom?

Dick:
Yes, the broom.

Alice:
> I'll tell him. And thank you for making the place look so clean. [PAUSE] And neat. [PAUSE] And tidy. [PAUSE] It'll help to keep the rats away.

Puss:
> [aside to Audience] I do not believe it!

Dick:
> [moving off] Well, good luck with the rats.

[As Dick and Alice move off, Puss erupts into another mewing mime in which she tries to get across that between Dick and her they could deal with any rats. Dick and Alice watch bemused. At last Puss stops, exhausted. PAUSE.]

Dick:
> Like I said, good luck with the rats. Goodbye.

Alice:
> Goodbye.

Puss:
> Oh, for goodness sake! Here I was giving an Oscar-winning performance making it so clear that a pea-brained pea could understand. And you two just stand there! Don't you realise I have a plan?

Dick:
> [shocked] But you can talk!

Puss:
> And your point is?

Alice:
> That you can talk!

Puss:
> Ye-es. And?

Dick:
> You can talk!

Puss:
> Look, can we get past the 'you can talk' bit. The audience will start getting restless. They've been patient up to now, but not for much longer, I bet.

... [And Puss takes over as the obvious brains of the outfit and incidentally explains how it came to pass that she can talk!]

The key elements here are the PAUSES. Getting the people playing Dick and Alice to have the confidence to wait a significant amount of time is fundamental to making the scene work. What is not being said is clear. Dick and Alice like each other at first sight and we all want it to develop, don't we? 'Oh, yes, we do!'

Playing romantic scenes can be difficult.

> 'It didn't mark me for life. A lot more embarrassing things have happened in my life. But it was very awkward at the time. I only ever met Rosie in the panto, and I didn't really know her at all. But we got through it.'
> [James Russ, aged 17, as Robin Hood]

The Hero and his Gang – Worship and Infatuation

The relationship between Dick and Alice in 'Dick Whittington' is genuinely innocent. In 'The Grand Old Duke of York' (which is not to be confused with 'The Grand Old Duchess of York' – a very different panto altogether) the relationship between a trio of upper-class teenage sisters, Melody, Harmony and Symphony and Charlie Chizzlewick, a jobless wanderer, is based on a significant misunderstanding, not that that stops the characters from having a good time.

Charlie enters dramatically to save the sisters from the attentions of a gang of Baddies.

Photo: Melody, Harmony and Symphony, in costumes created by themselves, with Charlie.

Now read on...

Charlie:
> [to Melody, Harmony & Symphony] It's all right, my ladies, they've gone. [The trio are in delighted shock unable to speak.] Might I ask who you are? [to Melody] My lady? [Melody is speechless.] You must be Miss Tongue-tied? [Melody dissolves into giggles. To Harmony] My lady? [Harmony can only giggle.] And you are Miss Giggler? [to Symphony] And you, my lady? [Symphony sighs and swoons.] You must be Miss Swooner [The trio laugh.]

Melody:
> You're him, aren't you? [to sisters] It is him, isn't it?

Symphony:
> No doubt about it. It's him all right.

Harmony:
> And here we are, together. Him and Us! [more giggles]

Melody:
> We've seen all your films. [Charlie is totally confused.]

Harmony:
> Every single one of them.

Symphony:
> We saw you as Sir Winalot in 'The Revenge of the White Knight'. [Sisters sigh.]

Harmony:
> As Lord Lindisfarne in 'Murder at Midnight'. [She sighs.]

Symphony:
> But best of all when you were...
> [to sisters] Remember?

Harmony:
> Oh, yes, when you were... [All sisters sigh.]

Charlie:
> When I was...?

Melody:
> You know.

Harmony:
> You must know.

Symphony:
> Of course he knows. How could he not know?

[Charlie is at a loss.]

Melody:
> When you were Suleiman, the Sheikh of Araby, in

'Darkness in the Dunes' and you flung Princess Pashmina onto the back of a camel and rode off with her into the sunset. [Sisters melt.]

Charlie:
: [about to explain] But...

Melody:
: Don't say a thing.

Harmony:
: We understand.

Charlie:
: You do?

Symphony:
: Yes, we do. You're here in York, incognito.

Charlie:
: In-cog-what?

Symphony:
: Incognito.

Melody:
: Under cover.

Harmony:
: In secret.

Melody:
: [explaining to sisters] Trying to avoid the paparazzi.

Harmony:
: The celebrity stalkers.

Symphony:
: And all those pathetic fans!

Melody:
: But your secret is safe with us.

Symphony:
: Our lips are sealed.

Harmony:
: We won't tell a soul that Suleiman, the Sheikh of Araby is here in York!

Melody & Symphony:
: Shhh!

[PAUSE]

Charlie:
: That's the ticket! Let's keep the fact that Suleiman, the Sheikh of...[forgets]

Melody, Harmony & Symphony:
   Araby!
Charlie:
   Yes, let's keep that as our secret. OK? [All sisters mime zipping their lips.] Now where were we? Oh, yes. Those thieves! Are you all, all right.
Melody:
   Yes, thanks to you, I'm quite safe.
Harmony:
   [not wanting to be overlooked] I'm quite safe, too.
Symphony:
   And me. But I could be safer!
Charlie:
   [referring to the gang he has driven off] Who were they?
Melody:
   Thieves!
Harmony:
   Robbers!
Symphony:
   Bounders!
Harmony:
   Brigands!
Melody:
   Vagabonds!
Symphony:
   [unable to think of another term] Err...
[PAUSE]
Melody:
   Have you been in York before?
Charlie:
   I've only just arrived.
Melody:
   I think we should introduce ourselves properly. I'm the Grand Old Duke's ward, Melody.
Harmony:
   And I'm the Grand Old Duke's ward, Harmony.
Symphony:
   And I'm the Grand Old Duke's ward, Symphony.
Charlie:
   Melody? Harmony? Symphony? Such lovely names.

Melody, Harmony & Symphony:
   [giggle] Thank you.
Charlie:
   The Grand Old Duke's very lucky to have three such pretty wards.
[More giggling]
Melody:
   And what do we call you? After all we can't call you Suleiman or Lord Lindisfarne, can we?
Charlie:
   No, I don't suppose you can. Call me Charlie Chizzlewick. At your service.
Melody:
   [playing along] And what are you doing in York,... Charlie?
Charlie:
   Looking for work. I'm willing to try anything.
Harmony:
   Anything?
Charlie:
   Anything.
Harmony:
   How good are you at marching?
Charlie:
   What?
Symphony:
   Left right. Left right [demonstrates]
Charlie:
   [marching] Left right? Left right?
Harmony:
   [applauds] Bravo! Well done!
Charlie:
   [smug] Thanks. Do you think so?
Melody:
   Some can never do it; but you're a born marcher. We'll have a word with the Grand Old Duke. He's always looking for more soldiers.
Harmony:
   He should have 10,000, but there are always some off sick or on holiday.

Symphony:
He never seems to have quite enough.
Charlie:
Wow! I've been in York less than a day and I'm already in the Grand Old Duke's Army. Who'd've thought it?
Melody:
Once we tell him how you saved us, [Sisters sigh.] he'll want you for sure.
Harmony:
He'll do anything for us.
Symphony:
By the way, can you sing?
Charlie:
Pardon?...

[...and before very long, Charlie is Commander-in-Chief of The Grand Old Duke's army.]

In the above scene we have some of the stock elements of any panto – misunderstandings, good luck, success achieved against the odds – all against a background of adoration.

There are many other forms for the relationship between Heroes or Heroines and their Gang of Goodies. But the poor man/boy/girl/woman who achieves against all the odds by inspiring others in the struggle for Good against the Baddies is central to most panto stories.

The Villain and the Villainess

The Baddies also express love and affection, but in unwholesome (if humorous) ways. Not for them the warm-hearted glow arising from a genuine care for another human being. They are in love – with the acquisition of Wealth or Power or preferably both Wealth and Power and in extreme amounts. Not so much a case of the more the merrier, but the most the merriest!

The Evil Couple are an item, being two sides of the same coin, singing from the same song sheet. One of them is the nominal leader, but that can change throughout a panto.

Colourful (if strange) terms of endearment are often used. Phrases such as 'my little lark's vomit surprise', 'my very own chocolate éclair with extra sprinkles', 'my dearest darkling', 'my saucy sweetmeat', all echoing the spirit of the Addams Family. They need each other, but are very likely to sell each other down the river when the going gets tough. Self-preservation is the order of the day. They don't waste any time developing their relationship as it is already well established. Their focus is entirely on 'The Plan' – how to get whatever it is they want. Let us turn to 'Robin Hood'. In the case of the Sheriff of Nottingham, he and his wife, Lady Thigh-Slapper, have power already, but want more wealth, much more wealth. Their first idea is to extract money from the Audience.

Sheriff:
> *[to Audience] Now harken you ill-begotten bumblers, you parasitical poltroons, it's Pay Day! [laughs] By which we mean, You Pay...*

Lady:
> *So we can Play!*

Sheriff:
> *I think that makes our positions perfectly clear. You are a gormless gang of numb-wit nobodies and we are fat cats who want more cream.*

Lady:
> *We are going to milk you all dry!*

Sheriff:
> *No point in protesting. It's udderly useless. Get it? Milk you dry. Udderly useless! [They laugh, as do the Guards.]*

Lady:
> *Don't go hiding your money under your mattresses, or under your floorboards.*

Sheriff:
> *We'll have it all, your mattresses and floorboards included. [being innocently reasonable] After all, if we don't get it, the [ultimate disgust] bankers will.*

Lady:
> *And do you really want that?*

Sheriff:
> Guards! [about Audience, to Guards] This lot look wealthier than the usual riff raff we have in Nottingham.

Lady:
> Squeeze 'em till you hear the pips squeak!

Sheriff:
> [to Audience] Give generously. It's all for a good cause - the very best of causes...

Sheriff/Lady:
> Us!

Sheriff:
> Think of the good you can do. [threatening] Or, if you prefer, think of the bad you can avoid.

Unfortunately for them the Audience is not in a giving mood. In spite of the best efforts of the Guards, they get nothing. Then, inspired by the approach of singing Lumberjacks, the Sheriff has an idea...

Sheriff:
> [to Lumberjacks] You... cut... down... trees. Interesting. Very interesting.

Lady:
> Is it, sweetums?

Sheriff:
> Yes, my little larks' vomit surprise. It is. Very interesting indeed! I feel the need to visit the forest.

Lady:
> You do? But you hate the forest.

Sheriff:
> Ax-actly! Come along, my very own crunchy nut cluster. There's gold in them thar trees! [encouraging speed] Chop chop! Geddit? Chop! Chop! Axes. Lumberjacks. [laughing] Oh, I'm such a card.

Lady:
> My very own Ace of Spades!

Sheriff:
> [correcting] King of Diamonds, dear. King of Diamonds.

[They exit on their way to set in motion the Sheriff's plan to replace Sherwood Forest with a Housing Development.]

Baddies have their very own cherished moments.

> 'I remember when the Knave gets his due come-uppance at the end and is threatened with jail or banishment or something similar, I threw myself down on to the floor and cried, incredulously, "I could be good...?" I don't think I was believed!'
> [Chris Fogg, who played opposite Lizzie Crane as Villain and Villainess, in 1998.]

📷 Photo: The Knave of Hearts with Mr Punch and Septicaemia.

Many Baddies can verge on being schizophrenic. Once or twice they have split completely. Read on to meet Boris the talking Toucan!

The Villains and their Cronies

No panto villain, even one with a horribly competent partner in crime at their side, can put The Plan into action without the help of their Yes-Men, cronies who will fawn and do their bidding, who demonstrate their 'love' with total dedication. Well, not exactly total. Even good Yes-Men know when to throw in the towel and make themselves scarce. In 'The Magic Cupboard' the Knave of Hearts (a different Knave from the one above) has a double-act of right-hand lads, Igor and Boris, as his cronies. He has been locked in 'The Magic Cupboard' for years with them until released accidentally by a gang of Apprentice Fairies...

> *Knave:*
> *[exiting the cupboard with Igor & Boris, to Audience] Ah-hah! The cupboard wasn't as empty or as ordinary as people thought, was it? Oh come on, you've waited long enough to boo someone. Is that the best you can do? Don't you realise? I am the Baddie!*
> *Igor & Boris:*
> *He is the Baddie!*
> *Knave:*
> *The best Baddie there is. I don't care who knows it. I'm Bad and I'm Proud.*
> *Igor:*
> *We're bad, too, Master.*

Boris:
But we'd love to be worse.
Knave:
You will, my horrors. You will.
Boris:
Be still my beating heart!
Igor:
Being bad is the best thing ever!
Knave:
[to Audience] As for you, you mealy-mouthed, pasty-faced, spotty-nosed, smelly-footed, feeble-minded pack of peasants, let us put you in the picture. [He clicks his fingers.]
Igor:
You have the great good fortune...
Boris:
The ultimate good luck...
Igor:
It's like Christmas and all your birthdays rolled into one.
Boris:
But better...
Igor:
Much better. Better even than discovering that the apple you've just eaten had a maggot in it!
Boris:
Ooh, maggoty apples are my favourite, especially ones with big, fat, grey, gooey ones. [Realises that Knave is waiting.] Sorry!
Igor:
Be upstanding.
Boris:
Be stand-upping.
Igor:
For Theobald Foxleigh-Struthers.
Boris:
The one and only...
Igor:
Celebrated...
Boris:
Distinguished...

Igor:
   Worldly-wise...
Boris:
   And wonderfully wicked!
Igor & Boris:
   Knave of Hearts!
Knave:
   [to Audience] Where's the ecstatic, enthusiastic and earth-shattering huzzahs? I demand cheers!
[Audience boos.]
Igor:
   No point in protesting. You're no match for him, the Mastermind of Crime.
Boris:
   Special subject – Nastiness.
Igor:
   Got a degree in Devilry, he has.
Knave:
   [to Igor & Boris] Make them cheer [Igor & Boris try but fail.] So that's how it's going to be, is it?...

[...and so the Knave proceeds with his plan to take over Nursery Rhyme Land.]

When we came to perform 'The Magic Cupboard' we ended up combining the roles of Igor and Boris. But as a challenge to the teenage lad who was playing both parts we made Boris a puppet toucan that 'spoke'. What?! ... You had to be there. It was very, very funny and suited the lad down to the ground.

'Favourite role? The Toucan. Definitely! That was two parts originally, and Ryan didn't wanna do it. And I said I'd do `em both. I don't know why. Don't think I was even thinking about the toucan, I was thinking about playing a split personality and being absolutely mental. I would love to be that Toucan again!'
[Alex Gibbons, who was that teenage lad.]

Photo: Theobald Foxleigh-Struthers, with Igor and Boris, his Toucan.

Double Acts

The chief Baddies can be called double acts. But here I am thinking more of pairings in the mould of Laurel & Hardy, Morecombe & Wise, French & Saunders, and the like. They are never evil, power-crazed Baddies, although some might verge towards badness. They bicker. They compete. But they need each other and can't get along without their other half. It is often this pairing who resort to the rat-a-tat of one line jokes, the older the better. Boris and Igor, above, are an extreme example. We have met another couple earlier, Tweedledum and Tweedledee, which were parts written for younger children. In 'Ali Baba and The Forty Thieves', our first panto, there was Mustafa Phag and Ali Beye, a pair of incompetent detectives. We first meet them when they back on to stage from different places in a mysterious fashion and bump into each other…

> *Mustafa & Ali:*
> *[turning to each other, wary] Hello, hello, hello. What's going on `ere then? [They both whip round to see.] What! Where?*
>
> *Mustafa:*
> *Hold it!*
>
> *Ali:*
> *Hold what!*
>
> *Mustafa:*
> *Look. Just hang on a second.*
>
> *Ali:*
> *Show me a second and I'll do my best. [Ali makes to exit.]*
>
> *Mustafa:*
> *You're behaving in a highly suspicious manner. There's been a report of a band of thieves and brigands nearby and you fit the description. I'm going to have to lock you up.*
>
> *Ali:*
> *What's the charge?*
>
> *Mustafa:*
> *No charge. It's all part of the service. I'll have you know that I'm Special Undercover Detective Phag, Mustafa Phag.*

Ali:
> Really. Well, that makes two of us.

Mustafa:
> Is your name Mustafa Phag, too?

Ali:
> No. I'm a Special Under-the-Bedclothes Detective, as well. The name's Beye, Ali Beye.

Mustafa:
> [suspicious] Oh, yes? Where were you born?

Ali:
> Right here in Cairo.

Mustafa:
> Which part?

Ali:
> All of me, stupid.

Mustafa:
> That's your story.

Ali:
> And I'm sticking to it.

Mustafa:
> Well, mind where you put your feet. Those camels really should clear up after themselves.

Ali:
> [taking Mustafa into his confidence] I'm on the look out for a band of thieves and brigands.

Mustafa:
> I told you that!

Ali:
> What?

Mustafa:
> I'm looking for a band of thieves and brigands.

Ali:
> You are?

Mustafa:
> Yes.

Ali:
> Me, too. Who'd've thought it?

Mustafa:
> Look, seeing there are two of us...

Ali:
> Phew! That's a relief. I thought I was seeing double.

Mustafa:
> You need glasses.

Ali:
> But I'm already wearing glasses.

Mustafa:
> In that case I need glasses... Look, why don't we split up?

Ali:
> [emotional, grabs Mustafa] But we must give our relationship a chance!

Mustafa:
> [pushes Ali away] You check over there, and I'll check over here.

Ali:
> That's what I was going to say.

Mustafa:
> [checking script, stepping out of character] No, I think you'll find it was my line.

[They exit.]

[Two of the 40 Thieves, Nasim and Wasim, cross stage with swag.]

Nasim:
> My brother's just opened a shop.

Wasim:
> Really? What's he doing?

Nasim:
> Six months. He opened it with a crowbar.

[They exit.]

[Mustafa and Ali re-enter, crossing.]

Mustafa:
> See anything?

Ali:
> Do you notice a change in me?

Mustafa:
> No. Why?

Ali:
> I've just swallowed a penny.

[They exit.]

[Two more of the 40 Thieves, Najma and Wajma, cross stage with swag.]

Najma:
   I hear your dad's cut the legs off his bed.
Wajma:
   He wants to lie low for a while.
[They exit.]
[Mustafa and Ali re-enter, crossing.]
Ali:
   I'm getting hungry.
Mustafa:
   What do you like best in sandwiches?
Ali:
   Truncheon meat.
[They exit.]
[Two more of the 40 Thieves, Walid and Rashid, cross stage with swag.]
Walid:
   I've not seen old Jamil around for a while.
Rashid:
   Haven't you heard? He stole two and half miles of elastic.
Walid:
   No!
Rashid:
   He's been put away for a long stretch.
[They exit.]
[Mustafa and Ali re-enter and stop.]
Ali:
   Hey, Mustafa. I've been thinking.
Mustafa:
   [aside to Audience] That's not good news.
Ali:
   Do you know why we can't find any of those desert thieves and brigands?
Mustafa:
   No. Why not?
Ali:
   Because they're using camel-flage...[laughs] Geddit?
[Mustafa hits him mercilessly!]
Mustafa:
   There's no point searching round here...

> *[The 40 Thieves cross stage behind them one by one. Audience 'behind you' business. Plenty of adlibbing from Ali and Mustafa but they never see anything and give up. Thieves all exit.]*
>
> *Ali:*
> *[referring to the large watch worn by Mustafa]* What's the time?
>
> *Mustafa:*
> Time to check the forest.
>
> *Ali:*
> I've been meaning to ask. *[points to watch]* What is that?
>
> *Mustafa:*
> I was given it by the local residents in recognition of my sterling work.
>
> *Ali:*
> *[dubious]* Oh yes?
>
> *Mustafa:*
> Yes. It's my Neighbourhood Watch!...Now come on.
> *[They exit.]*

This is how it was written. How was it performed?

> 'We were constantly interrupting one another and finishing each other's lines off alternately. Consequently, I got mixed up differentiating between those lines I was supposed to say and those lines that were for Tim. Fortunately Tim knew both parts and so was able to switch at will in order to accommodate whatever I might happen to come out with!'
> [Chris Fogg, who was Mustafa Phag (or maybe Ali Beye) alongside his son, Tim.]

This account gives evidence of a claim I make elsewhere: that children, especially teenagers, often give the strongest, most dependable and stage-savvy performances of all.

In the scene above not only do we have the Double Act of Mustafa and Ali, but mini examples of the D.A. in the pairs of thieves.

Another form of the Double Act is a version of the 'Ugly Sisters routine', an example of the 'competitive Dames' we have talked about above. In 'The Princess and the Dragon' we have the Ladies Sylvestra Sourgrapes and Clothilde Crabapple, who as their names suggest are sharp and positively acid at times. And naturally they are man-hungry. We hear them before we see them. Princess Damson (the ultimate Goodie) is on stage to make the introductions.

> Sylvestra:
> *[offstage] You look like a toad on a bad hair day!*
> Clothilde:
> *[offstage] And you look like a toad on a bad hair day that's been run over by a herd of elephants.*
> Princess:
> *[to Audience] You are about to meet my charming aunts. Fasten your seat belts, you're in for a bumpy ride. You have been warned.*
> *[Clothilde & Sylvestra burst on stage, unaware of the Audience.]*
> Clothilde:
> *You look a sight! A waste disposal site!*
> Sylvestra:
> *The mudpack I gave you improved your appearance. But then it fell off.*
> Clothilde:
> *I'm the sort of woman men look twice at.*
> Sylvestra:
> *That's because they can't believe it the first time!*
> Clothilde:
> *The last time you had a facial they had to call in heavy earth-moving equipment.*
> Sylvestra:
> *Last year at Halloween they asked you to take your mask off because you were scaring the children. But you weren't wearing one!*
> Princess:
> *Lady Crabapple. Lady Sylvestra.*
> Clothilde & Sylvestra:
> *Don't interrupt!*

Princess:
>Maybe you haven't noticed, [indicates the Audience] but we have guests.

[Clothilde & Sylvestra double take before approaching the Audience at speed.]

Clothilde:
>Not just guests, dear.

Sylvestra:
>Have you noticed?

Clothilde:
>Of course, I have.

Sylvestra:
>Many of them...

Clothilde:
>Are men.

[They dissolve into girlish giggles.]

Sylvestra:
>Let me introduce myself. I am the ravishing Lady Sylvestra Sourgrapes.

Clothilde:
>[aside] The bloom of freshness rubbed off years ago. [announcing] And I am the pulchritudinous Lady Clothilde Crabapple.

Sylvestra:
>[aside, knowingly] And we all know what they say about crabs!

Clothilde:
>We are sisters to her Majesty, Queen Peardrop.

Sylvestra:
>More importantly, we are young, rich and...available!

Princess:
>Aunties...

Sylvestra:
>Shhh! This is an opportunity not to be missed. [referring to a man in the Audience] Oh look, that gorgeous hunk of manhood just rolled his eyes at me.

Clothilde:
>Well, roll them back so he can get a good eyeful of me!

Sylvestra:
>[to the same man] You naughty, naughty man. I know exactly what you're thinking...and the answer is YES!

Clothilde:
 Yes?
Sylvestra:
 Yes! Yes! Yes! Saturday afternoon at 3 o'clock. And I'll wear white.
Princess:
 What are you talking about?

Sylvestra:
>*Our wedding, silly.*

Clothilde:
>*[to Sylvestra] If I was married to you, I'd poison your food.*

Sylvestra:
>*[to Clothilde] If I was married to you, I'd eat it!*

Princess:
>*We should be making final arrangements for the Ball.*

Sylvestra:
>*The Ball! Oh, what shall I wear?*

Clothilde:
>*Something in black. Plastic. Suitable for a sack of rubbish like yourself.*

Sylvestra:
>*You're just jealous. After all, I've got legs to die for.*

Clothilde:
>*Call them legs. They're more like matchsticks. No. Not quite. They are sticks all right, but they certainly don't match.*

Sylvestra:
>*I could have been the world's greatest ballerina.*

Clothilde:
>*[to Princess] Only two things stopped her.*

Princess:
>*What?*

Clothilde:
>*Her feet! [to Audience] But enough about her. There's always little me. I'm free.*

Sylvestra:
>*To a good home.*

Clothilde:
>*[hurt] Oh, how could you?*

Sylvestra:
>*Easy, my dear Clottie. I have a talent to abuse...*

[And so the bickering cements the bond that binds the sisters together. The Audience feels sympathy for any man unlucky enough to be snared by one or other of them. In the case of this panto, General Greengage walks into the trap with his eyes shut. Foolish man.]

Let's hear from the Lovely Lady Sylvestra Slopbucket.

> 'Dave's bust was either two large balloons or footballs, and his eyelashes were the most ridiculously long and curled ones. A photograph of me in that costume and in that character went up in the staff coffee room at work and the practice manager put up 'Guess Who?' And no-one guessed who it was.'
> [John Horne]

And not to be left out, let's hear from the equally Lovely Lady Clothilde Crabapple.

> 'I only dressed up as a woman once, in not exactly colour-coordinated, discrete, understated attire. And I recall my kids afterwards telling me how open-mouthed, gob-smacked they were as their terribly pc father, responsible public servant etc, seemed to have deserted all common decency and taste. To which I retorted: "Yes, and my partner-in-crime other lady was, of course, none other than the local GP..."'
> [Dave Crane]

Aside Three – Crowd Scenes

First a reminder: Everyone in our pantos is a named character and has a distinct role to play. They are not there to fill up the stage as nameless village folk and the like. And now we need to agree on what a crowd is. How many does it take to make a crowd? In fact, is size the determining factor? My answer to the second question is 'No'. A small stage or performance area can appear crowded with relatively few people on it.

Photo: The Grand Old Duke of York's Army proudly wearing hats made by villagers.

If a scene has 15 people in it, such as scenes with the army in 'The Grand Old Duke of York', it can get crowded, but each character is an individual vocal contributor to the action and helps move the plot along. This therefore in my book is not a crowd scene.

I feel that a crowd is any group of characters who are observers of and commentators on a scene, rather than being the makers of it. Almost any character can become a crowd member at some point. As we will see in 'Chases' on pages 132-133, even Robin Hood and Snow White can for a while become part of the crowd watching and wondering about the scene being played out in front of them.

From a writing point of view, the practicality of staging such scenes needs to be thought through. The relationship of the members of the crowd with the characters they are observing or commenting on is to be worked on during rehearsals. During the writing process, the crowd is referred to as 'All'. Here is an example from 'The Grand Old Duke of York' when the Duke enters with a lot of other characters. He is reading a copy of the Baddies' plan that has fallen into his hands.

Duke:
   [reading] Oh, no!
All:
   Oh, yes.
Duke:
   [reading more] Oh, no!
All:
   Oh, yes.
Duke:
   [reading more] Oh no!!
All:
   Oh, yes.
Sergeant Stickleback:
   [to Corporal Cod] Slow reader, isn't he?
Cod:
   Sure is.
Duke:
   [finishing reading] Oh, no, no, no, no, no!
All:
   Oh, yes, yes, yes, yes, yes!
Duke:
   Baron Grabbit is planning to do the dirty.
All:
   We know.

Duke:
>   *He's going to give me the chop.*
All:
>   *We know.*
Duke:
>   *To cut me off in my prime.*
All:
>   *We know.*
Duke:
>   *To...*
All:
>   *[interrupting] We know!*
Duke:
>   *We're all doomed!...*

[It looks really bad, but never fear the Baron's days are numbered.]

Aside Four – Songs and Music

As has been said when talking about deciding on a script [see: Act One: Scene Three, pages 18-19], professionally written pantos often include a lot of songs and live music. Now if your community has an accompanist, who can inspire confidence and train the cast to sing the songs, that is great. If not, what can you do? Well, discarding the songs from a script is one route to go down, but this can weaken the panto significantly.

We are not a choir. Our casts are full of unconfident singers. Sometimes our original scripts don't have any songs at all. Other times we have a big choral number and nothing more. In 'Robin Hood' we surprised ourselves and had no less than four different songs. When we sing, how do we decide what to sing?

- We pick an old familiar tune that is well known or very easy to pick up.

- We rewrite the lyrics to suit our panto.

- We usually have characters sing as a group in unison because that helps build confidence.

- All songs are to be sung with gusto and often really raucously! We have rarely tried for anything truly tuneful.

From a performance point of view I feel that with unconfident singers it has often been better for them to sing without accompaniment. Why? Maybe they feel more reluctant to let rip if they have one ear on the music. We adopt a principle that the songs we pick are chorus numbers and need to be belted out. Never mind the singing quality, go for broke and knock the audience off their chairs! It is, in short, the spirit of sing-along pub songs, but in a panto.

I suppose you could go down the karaoke route, singing to a recorded backing track. But as I have no experience of that I cannot comment.

As for live music, all I can say is what we have done over the years. We have never been able to call upon the services of the kind of musician who can extemporise and who can accompany anyone singing in any key. We have had people happy to accompany a popular song or two, but they would not have wanted to play a full score. So as a result we have done original pantos without any live music, merely using non-copyright recorded music instead.

Here is a possible solution: Maybe a member of the cast has a talent you can use. Maybe a child can play the recorder or the piano.

> 'There was one production where I had to make an exit through the audience to the lobby, and from there straightaway sit at the piano to play quite a plonky version of 'Teddy Bears' Picnic' for the opening music of the following scene. I remember this made me feel very important as a little girl.'
> [Rosie Crane]

Aside Five – Recycling

Once you have written and/or directed your first panto there is no need to start completely from scratch if you are doing your second, or third, or nth. Never forget that your audience have only spent a couple of hours immersed in your panto-world. If you choose to do another panto twelve months later, how much will your audience remember from the year before? Not much, is the answer. And if, like us, the gap is greater, it is safe to say that of the script your audience will remember nothing. They will recall the fun they had, and that is about all. Use this to your advantage. Recycle favourite jokes. We now have some that appear almost every time! Recycle bits of dialogue and parts of scenes with minor tweaks and changes. We have even recycled the core of whole scenes by making gender changes and/or introducing a new character or two. After several years, no one remembers anything! Even regular cast members forget what was in the panto before last. This might not be the case for the regular Director and/or Writer, but turned to their advantage it helps reduce the need to be 'new' every time.

Aside Six – Casting

You have worked with the characters and their relationships. You have worked out what The Plan is – what the Baddies intend to do to turn your panto world topsy turvy. You've done all you can to get a good script. You now need to cast it. If you are very lucky, there is a perfect marriage between the people who want to be in the panto and the parts you have to offer. However, things are rarely like that.

You might realise, that in spite of your best efforts, there are no matches between certain roles and the list of names you are looking at. In that case you have these options:

- Go back to the community and try to recruit again.

- Change the gender of a certain character. So Abanazar becomes Abanellie!

- Turn a single character into two or more. So The Evil Witch becomes a Trio of Witches.

- Conversely turn two or more characters into one as we did with Igor and Boris in 'The Magic Cupboard' as has been mentioned above.

You will also have more people stepping forward at a late stage wanting to be in it. One of the reasons for doing the panto at all is to encourage involvement and to help people develop new skills, so you do not say: 'Sorry. Too late.' You are creative. 7 Dwarfs become 14. You add to your Market Traders, your Fairies, your Soldiers, Pirates and Thieves. You can also create a whole new scene. As a result ghouls, spooks and ghosts now occupy Aladdin's Cave before he arrives.

Aside Seven – A warning (though that might be too strong)

I have never used an audition process, because it smacks of taking the whole project too seriously and would definitely put off more people than it would attract. As a result, if someone totally unknown to me as a performer steps forward I have learned not to give them a leading part. Let them prove their worth. In the early days I took people's word that they had some experience and cast them accordingly. In some cases that proved to be a mistake. But never forget that the reason for doing a community panto is to involve as many people as possible; this means using people across the talent range.

Aside Eight – Availability

Availability is a major concern when it comes to deciding who plays what. You look for a night when the Director is available (bearing in mind that he/she attends every minute of every rehearsal unlike anyone else until very late on in the schedule). You decide that Friday is the night for rehearsals (no school day the next day/ end of working week/ venue available...), but X has another regular commitment. In that case X is offered a smaller part than otherwise he/she might have had. Z can make

Fridays, but doesn't get home from work till after 7.30pm, so it's hard for Z to be in any scenes with the youngest children who rehearse from 6.00 to 7.00pm. You get the picture.

Availability of the rehearsal space must also be considered. What other activities are on and when? There is also the matter of cost. Is there a hiring fee for the space? If so, how is that being funded? We will come to financial matters on pages 85-86.

Where were we? Casting the panto. You sit. You 'um' and 'ahh'. You toss a coin or two. You make your decisions and you have a cast. You let them know who's playing who, and that rehearsals will start soon. In the meantime you will get a script to them.

Aside Nine – Providing scripts

If you are using a set of scripts from the public library, you have no problem. If, on the other hand, you are producing the script 'in house', you either have to print or photocopy it (or sections of it for the smaller roles). This can be costly. Or you can email it for the cast themselves to print off. I have come to favour emailing. It's one of the costs which cast members are willing to absorb. After all, members of any club or hobbyists in general are prepared to subsidise their activity in some way. Of course, even today there are people without email or printers. They need pre-printed scripts.

ACT THREE

Including: Let's start with Costumes. Talking about Set and Scenery.

Act Three – Scene setting

It is now time to sit down with the backstage crew and those who are going to work with you to make the panto a success.

Act Three – Scene One: Let's start with Costumes

> 'My poor Mum always probably waited with baited breath of what the latest costume she had to construct out of old curtains or netting or from adaptations of those costumes used previously!'
> [Eleanor Dunhill]

For many cast members costumes are the number one concern. They want to look good. They want to look very different from what they normally do. And a costume can and does turn a regular performance into something special. Over 20 years and 10 pantos we have had just two Costume Chiefs. Incredible. They have given their all for our shows!

You sit down with the Costume Designer/Maker-in-Chief – who is one of the team of stalwarts you recruited right at the start – and go through the list of characters. You present your ideas. She presents hers. You doodle and sketch, but more than anything you encourage her to go Over The Top (OTT). Never forget that 'This is not dressmaking'. The costumes are to be looked at from a distance. They don't need to have longevity built in. Costumes are about character, impact, colour, and in some cases 'the extreme'. If you have a Dame, she needs to be dressed brazenly in the most outrageous fashion – with probably more than one outfit. She is loud, in your face, clashing, fun, the spirit of carnival. By contrast the costumes of Baddies need to shout "We Are Bad!" – black, red, silver, gold, spiky.

You might try to borrow costumes from the local Am Dram Society. You might think that costuming some characters in basic T-shirts and tights with homemade add-ons is suitable. In that case you buy them. Visit charity shops for outfits that can be used as the basis for a costume. You should hire certain costumes that would take too much time, effort and money to make, eg: a pantomime cow. You might have a costume store already, which you can raid and adapt whatever you find, pressing old costumes into new forms. But it is most likely that you will need to make costumes in number from scratch. Also, making results in involving more people and that is what a community panto is about – the involvement of as many people as possible. The sharing of skills. The giving of time and energy. You might well put out a request to the community for unwanted material – cotton sheets can be dyed, curtains can be cut up. This is a free resource to draw on. If you are buying material, go for cheap and cheerful, material with a shine to it, ends of roll and oddments, and see it you can get a deal. But shopping means spending money.

That is what I have to say about costumes. But what does our current Costume Designer/Maker-in-Chief, have to say? Here are her bullet points:

- 'Some cast members can sort their own costumes. Some cannot.

- Don't assume that a female partner can produce a costume for her husband.

- Be sensitive/diplomatic to cast's feelings when discussing dress sizes.

- Beware of general appeals for materials. You might get a great deal of unusable stuff, which you then have to dispose of.

- During initial discussions with cast members, if he/she says he/she has certain items, ask to see them a.s.a.p. to be sure you are both on the same wavelength.

- Know any existing costumes used in previous pantos. Rotate and/or adapt them where it is appropriate. Don't use costumes in consecutive pantos.

- Aim to have costumes ready 3 weeks before Dress Rehearsal.

- Make time at rehearsals for costume fitting. It's not always possible to meet with cast other than at rehearsals.'

And finally:

- 'Be aware of a Director who does not wish to allocate rehearsal time for fittings and won't have talking going on during rehearsal.'
  [Rosemary Shepherd]

Now you know why they are called 'bullet' points. Yes, I know, I can be difficult!

Some cast members are able and willing to make their own costumes. Some do it with glee and great creativity. A case in point is Hilary Baker, whose costumes have always been a tour de force!

📷 Photo: Mother Hubbard and Tom Piper.

What was Hilary's costume-making method?

> 'You always give me a rough idea, and then I would just cut it out. And do it. I dunno how I did it, but I thoroughly enjoyed doing it. I never measured nothing! Or pinned it. I just loved the fantasy of it all. The worse the costume is, the better!'
> [Hilary Baker]

Now, at last, to financial matters.

Aside Ten – Money

Let's talk about how we can afford to do our pantos. We've been putting it off, but we knew we were going to have to do it sometime, so why not now. We can't have Fun without Funds (Ho! Ho!). If your group/community already has a kitty, perhaps all you need to do is set a budget for costumes, scenery, venue hire and the like. But what can you do if you don't have a kitty?

- Ask your cast to pay for or provide their own costumes.
- Charge a 'membership fee'.
- Stage a fundraising event – eg: coffee morning, jumble sale.
- Look for sponsors.
- Seek a grant from a local source, eg: the village hall.
- Apply for funding from a recognised provider, eg: local authority, charity, etc. [This takes time and you cannot be sure of a successful outcome.]

In order to go through official channels in your search for funding you will need to be a formally constituted group, or attached to a formally constituted group. This means that you will have to have adopted a written constitution. This doesn't have to be a lengthy document, but it must set out your structure, your mission, and your policy. In short, it must say who you are, how you are organised and what you set out to do. This constitution needs to have been agreed to at an open meeting. You will need a minimum of three officers - a chairperson, a treasurer and a secretary. You will need to have a current bank account in your group's name with two nominated signatories. Even if you are not seeking funding, your group will need a bank account to receive income from ticket sales in the form of cash and, very likely, in cheques. You will also need to repay certain expenses incurred by the panto. A cheque book is a useful basic tool for this. Without it people are going to have to wait until cash begins to come in from ticket sales to be reimbursed.

When we first did pantos we received a £100 'seed grant', a loan from the Village Hall Committee. This set a limit on our budget and we worked within it. It is amazing how creative you can be with relatively little. And rather than pay a hiring fee for the use of the Hall for each rehearsal, we agreed that the income from the performances would be shared; half to the Hall and half for us to build up resources and reduce the need for future grants. In this way we paid back the 'seed grant' and covered the Hall hire fees. In subsequent years the Hall Committee decided to direct their share of the income into buying stage lights and upgrading the sound system. This has improved the quality of production we can offer and also made the Hall more attractive to other users. [For Lighting and Sound, go to Act Seven, pages 161-168.] We are now completely self-funding for most things, but if cast members feel the need to develop their own costumes, they will fund that themselves or be given some small amounts of financial help.

Regarding potential outgoings you might need to pay for:

- hiring charges for venue/rehearsal space.
- performing rights' fees.
- printing scripts.
- photocopying promotional material, printing posters and tickets.
- paint and related art materials.
- hiring stage lights and sound system.
- set building material.
- stage make-up.

But costumes are (for us) by far the biggest expense - buying material and haberdashery and occasionally hiring. We want to know that 'the look' we want is one we can afford.

Act Three – Scene Two: Talking about Scenery and Set

You now sit with your other community creatives – the people who can paint and construct, frequently from little or nothing, and within the fixed limitations of the budget and the venue. Does your venue have offstage space in the wings or elsewhere for storage? Does it have any sort of permanent backdrop? Are you able to suspend scenery? In short, what can the venue offer you that you can use?

For me scenery is made up of the drops or cloths that hang at the back or at the sides of your performance area/stage. They provide a static backdrop. You might have more than one set of them, of course, and change them during the performance. In that case you need to build time into the show when it is running for that to happen. The Interval offers a good opportunity for this. You definitely need to have recruited someone with artistic ability to make the design, and then transfer the idea to canvas or sheeting or old curtaining or whatever material your scenery is made of.

You sit with your Scenery Artist and have a similar conversation to the one you have had with your Costume Designer/Maker-in-Chief. You have your ideas for the atmosphere you want to create – a forest, in a Chinese Market, on a Pirate Ship, outside a Castle. You've made a few doodles of your own. The scenery is there to give the audience a sense of place and give the scenes atmosphere. As with the Costume Designer, you then let the Artist get on with it. Even if you are a total control freak, you must delegate and let others be creative in their own way. In that way they will enjoy what they are doing and make their own contributions. Of course, you have every right to see their ideas, to review progress, to make suggestions, but never forget that this venture is a team effort.

The Scenery Artist then needs the space and materials to turn her/his ideas into a reality.

Over the years we have been able to call upon the talents of two local artists. In each case they have called upon members of Art Clubs that they have run or been members of to assist them.

Here are some dos and don'ts from Jenny Beck, Scenery Designer/Artist.

- Start early! As soon as the panto is decided upon, appeal for helpers for scenery, set and prop production.

- Another appeal! For unwanted water-based household paint which is fine to use on its own or with acrylic paints - the only absolute no is drawing with felt tip pens, as the ink will bleed through any subsequent layers of paint forever and ever.

- Also avoid fixing things with plastic-coated tape. It'll never be able to be painted over.

- If you are enlarging a design onto a backdrop, it is vastly quicker and easier on your arms to get someone to help with drawing the grid.

- Have a plan/small sketch of what is to be painted to show helpers, and have the basic design sketched out ready to paint.

- Save time and paint! Over the course of many pantos we have evolved into having 2 or 3 main backdrops with basic background scenes – woodland, stone wall (castle or baronial hall interior), fields and sky etc., which we re-use with different props and other elements made specifically for each production.

- Prop painting day. Have a special day with lots of groundsheets, tea and biscuits. Helpers come along dressed for mess and paint all the set and props (hopefully) in one day. Children love helping out with this and often come up with some brilliant ideas.

📷 Photo: Painting part of the cottage.

Jenny has mentioned set, so let's look at that. Set is made up of all the bits and pieces (some of which are called 'flats') that are able to come on and go off during the performance as and when they are needed. They add to the sense of place created by the scenery. For example: a freestanding giant tree against the forest backdrop, or a little cottage set against a rural backdrop. You might also need a giant mangle for Widow Twankey to use, a cave with a sliding door for Aladdin, a giant shoe for Mother Hubbard's children to live in, a magic cupboard to hide in. Whatever it is, these pieces of set are fundamental to the storyline, and the panto cannot happen without them. They are not hire-able or purchase-able. They need to be made and someone needs to make them. You cannot begin rehearsing until you are sure such requests are possible.

📷 Photo: The finished cottage on stage.

A simple and straightforward approach to set building is best.

> 'When I was doing the set making it was a bit rough and ready. It were nothing too special! `Cos when the others took over it was lovely. But it done the trick. Made out of cardboard and rough old bits of wood. Just nailed together. But it worked, didn't it? We `ad no plan at all. We just went on and knocked it up whatever we thought.'
> [Mike Baker]

So you arrange to meet up with your Construction Team, which is usually a group of blokes who like a challenge and can wield a power tool.

You meet them at the venue with your list of things to make and with doodles of what you envisage with a few rough measurements. Now it is up to them. If you have an engineer on board, he will want everything down to the last 'thou' or millimetre. Let him make the mangle that must work and 'consume' people, or the fireplace that must revolve. You might have some DIYers - men who have all the tools, and like to use them. If so, again you are lucky.

A key message for them is that they are not installing a kitchen or making a bespoke item of furniture. This is panto. As long as whatever they are making looks good from a distance and survives to the end of the last night of performance, that is absolutely fine.

Photo: Painting scenery.

You encourage them above all to think 'lightweight'. Never forget sets have to be movable. They probably have to come on and go off during the show. So when it comes to materials we follow the approach used by set builders in our very first panto. They used 1in x 1in rough-cut timber battening (frequently off-cuts or gash) and sheet cardboard. Unfolded boxes in which white goods arrive or which are used by house removal companies, or sheets of the stuff disposed of by so many industrial enterprises are just the job. With these simple materials anything is possible. Easy to cut. Easy to fix with lightweight nails, tacks or even staples. Easy to paint. And you may find that being exact is not the right way. Read on:

'For one panto we made 'walls' that hanged over the beams above the stage. We'd make things and then have to alter them. We learned if you measure to the inch nothing is really level. So you've got to put it where you want it and mark it and work from there.'
[Sam Trott]

The Construction Team also has to solve the age-old problem of set storage. It's all very well having a fantastically made cave for Aladdin, but if it's in one piece, where can you put it when it's not in use during the panto? This is the kind of problem the constructors enjoy. Honestly. They spend hours debating the finer points of folds, hinges, flaps, assembly, disassembly and re-assembly. It must be just the same when IKEA designers are in conference. Panto is truly the home of 'flatpack' sets.

So we have Scenery and Set planned, designed and being made, but why stop there? Your venue is most likely a communal space – a Hall of some sort – why not bring your vision of your panto world down off the stage and into the 'auditorium'. For our panto, 'Robin Hood', we turned the Hall into Sherwood Forest. How? We draped the walls with loads of camouflage netting borrowed through Royal Marine contacts. Then we added real 'trees' supplied and installed by a local tree surgeon. The magical result invited the audience to enter the world of the panto as soon as they stepped through the door of the Hall, and further increased the sense of anticipation and excitement for both audience and cast. But naturally this type of transformation can only be installed a few days before the performances (possibly as late as the day before).

Aside Eleven – A word about 'stage levels'

Does your venue have a raised stage? If so, that is a significant bonus, as the audience's view will be much improved. If you don't have a raised stage, you can use stage blocks. You could perhaps borrow these from another venue, eg: the local school. If you have a raised stage with curtains, do you also have any usable stage area in front of them? If so, there is nothing stopping you staging Front of Curtain scenes. If there is no usable area out front, as we had for a few years, you can borrow some scaffolding with boards and build an extension up to stage level. This might sound challenging, but someone in your community will probably be able to do it or will know someone who can. Of course, this kind of extension can only be installed in the last few days of the rehearsal period if it reduces the use of the venue for other activities. After a few years of doing this, the Village Hall Chairman came up with a design for a permanent fold-down extension. Attached to the front lip of the permanent stage, this works like a giant gate leg table or lid in two sections. It now means that at every rehearsal we can use all of the available stage area – both in front of and behind the curtains. Training the cast to raise and lower it is part of Rehearsal Number One. Adults lift and children dart underneath to pull out and fix the legs. Call it 'team building', if you like.

For photographs of the procedure for erecting the stage extension, see Appendix II.

Full colour photographs are also available.

With or without a raised stage, any panto set gains from having different levels in it.

Blocks to sit on. Sets of steps to stand on. These help to add interest to the 'look' from the audience's point of view. Regarding steps, if the venue has a raised stage but no steps up to it from the auditorium this needs to be dealt with. Sets of steps extend the choice of entrances and exits and allow cast members to leave the stage and move among the audience.

Aside Twelve – A word about Exits and Entrances

> 'Which way did I go last time? Was it down those stairs? Or did I go behind the curtain. Andrew'll know. He'll tell me.'
> [Rod Bracher]

When it comes to plotting the flow of the panto, the Director wants to have as many ways on and off stage for the cast as are possible, and be certain of them before he/she starts the rehearsal process. The more routes there are for characters to enter and exit, the better. They offer choice, which makes for visual interest and helps the production to flow more slickly. In a panto with around 40 actors, getting them on and off can be like a military exercise. With a large number of routes characters can be exiting and entering at will. It also allows a stage full of characters to empty quickly, or conversely characters can rush on from all points, and an empty stage can become a busy one in a few moments. If the stage in the venue you are using has no backdrop with adequate space behind it, there is an immediate problem. If a character enters stage left, he must exit the same way. For, if he exits stage right, he has to wait in the wings as there is no way for him to get back to the stage left side without crossing the stage in full sight of the audience.

So this is what we feel is required to provide a minimum number of routes on and of stage.

- A backdrop, either permanent or temporary, either curtain or painted backdrop or painted flats with a gap behind it big enough for characters to cross the stage out of view.

- Four on-stage points where entrances and exits can be made. These are most likely upstage left and right, and downstage left and right.

- Two points where characters can enter or exit the stage from the auditorium, eg: by steps left and right.

For the purposes of panto the auditorium can often offer a much larger alternative 'stage' for some scenes. In this case any routes into the auditorium can be used for exits and entrances allowing for very busy, big scenes indeed. Here is an example from our production of 'Dick Whittington'. The auditorium became the merchant ship and the crew entered from everywhere they could. The audience realised that they were on board 'The Saucy Sal'. Unfortunately for them the Captain had 'crates' of cargo to load. [They were in fact large cardboard boxes from a recent house move in the village.] The crew now made the audience pass these boxes from the back of the hall to the stage at the front over their heads. Needless to say the scene wasn't as simple or as straightforward as that sounds when written down. It was instead semi-organised chaos and great fun.

> 'We were passing the cargo over the audience's heads and suddenly the audience were well-and-truly part of the cast. I think that the best shows are always those where – even if it's not through direct participation like that – the cast and the audience somehow become locked together in a joint enterprise.'
> [Brian Hesketh]

Another reason for having multiple routes, which include the auditorium, is that with them our enthusiasm for chases can be met. With chases we aim for the essence of farce [without the doors] – with entrances and exits happening all over the place, involving as many characters as possible travelling at comic speed. [For much more on Chases, go to Act Four: Scene Five, pages 132-133.]

INTERVAL

Time for a breather. Having got a script. Having got Costume, Set and Scenery making all started, it is time to start Rehearsals. For this there needs to be a Rehearsal Schedule so that everyone knows ahead of time when and where they are wanted, and to do what.

ACT FOUR

Including: Drawing up a Rehearsal Schedule. Managing Rehearsals. How to get a performance and a few basic bits of stagecraft or 'business'. Children on stage – How to get them to give of their best (and adults, too!). Chases.

Act Four – Scene One: Drawing up a Rehearsal Schedule

The first things to decide upon are the non-negotiable dates – the dates of the performance(s), when everything and everyone must be present and ready for 'show time'.

There is a common feeling that pantos are for Christmas time or soon after. We have never done that. Instead we have almost always picked a date the week before Easter (there or thereabouts). Even though Easter moves back and forth in the calendar and can be anything from the end of March to the middle of April, we decided that rehearsing during January, February, March and sometimes into April suits us. Cast members have been heard to say that it gives them something to focus on in the 'low' that often comes in the early weeks of a new year – in the post-Christmas lull, when the weather is often depressing and darkness comes all too early.

There are some theatrical groups who rehearse for many months more. That definitely isn't for us. To get such long term commitment from busy people is not on. People here are happiest making a concerted effort over a shorter time period than stretching it out almost endlessly.

And why the week before Easter? So that people can move on with their lives as the schools begin to break up for holidays. Rehearsals take our cast from the depth of winter to the brink of spring.

> 'On a winter night, going out when it's dark – it's good timing. It'd be totally wrong in summer.'
> [Robert Fooks]

Another thing you need to think about at the outset is the number of performances you plan to give. This depends on the following factors: How big is your venue and how many tickets do you think you can sell? We regularly sell c280 tickets. Our Hall has space to seat a maximum of 150. As a result we do two performances. When we began, 20 years ago, we thought about doing one show on a Friday evening and another on the Saturday evening. But this excluded a lot of the very youngest children who we wanted to see our show from coming. There was also a number of our oldest villagers who wanted to come, but were unhappy being away from home in the dark. Our decision was to do two performances on the Saturday of choice, a Matinee at 2.30pm and an Evening performance at 7.30pm. This gave us two great audiences - the first more child-filled, the second much more adult. Another benefit of having two-shows-in-a-day is that everyone in the cast and backstage is geared up for action and there is no letting up. One whole day is dedicated to panto.

Once our performance date is fixed, there are three other dates, which we always fix working back from the date of our performances. In reverse order they are the dress rehearsal, which is often on the day immediately before our performances, and the technical run-through, which is two or three days before that. It is chiefly designed, as its name suggests, to fix and sort out lighting and sound, but is in fact a full-run without costumes. The last date, which we fix from the outset, is usually a week before our performances where we do our first full run through with full set and scenery in place.

It may appear that by talking about our performances we are running before we have taken our first steps, but those last dates are the target to which we are aiming throughout the whole rehearsal period. It also provides delivery deadlines for everyone else working on the panto, particularly the costume, set and scenery makers.

We are now ready to draw up the schedule.

We have one major rehearsal day a week, Friday. And we have another day for smaller rehearsals as and when needed. As has been said the Director is the only person who has to be available for all rehearsals. Nobody else is called to all rehearsals – not until the last week to ten days.

Key rules for planning the schedule:

- Break your script up into small sections 3 to 4 pages long maximum.

- Decide ahead how long you think each section needs, anything from 20 minutes to an hour depending on its complexity and the number of characters.

- Draw up a schedule that calls groups of people for specific times, eg: All Lumberjacks from 7.00pm to 7.30pm.

- Children under 11 should be rehearsed early in a session, say 6.00 to 7.00pm.

- If you need to see a character/characters in more than one scene, try to group those scenes close together if at all possible.

- Rehearsing after 9.00pm is not really a good idea, although sometimes it is necessary.

- Never forget that rehearsals are a social occasion. Your cast are there because they want to be, not because they have to be.

The key message is "Don't have your cast sitting around wasting time." If you want them to be punctual, the Director must do the same. If a scene has not been fully rehearsed, but the time for the next scene's rehearsal has arrived, move on. You can always pick up where you had got to another time. It also allows the director the right to comment if a cast member is unpunctual.

If you can rehearse the script in order so much the better, but be prepared not to. Tackling in a single session all the different scenes in which a certain group of characters appears together can be a good idea.

So you draw up your schedule taking the above into account. It is not easy. If we have a 12-week rehearsal period, we tend to do a first schedule to cover the first 6 weeks only. By the end of that period we should have set the whole panto (= run through the scenes, fixed all exits and entrances, plotted all the movement, begun working on characterisation and performance). We review progress, see what still needs to be done and plan accordingly. Our second schedule takes us through the rest of the rehearsal period all the way to 'show time'. [See Appendix IV 'Full Rehearsal Schedule' for 'Robin Hood'.]

Act Four – Scene Two: Managing rehearsals

'It's amazing watching the rehearsals – it looks like mayhem! You think: "How on earth is this ever gonna work?" And it does!! It's like some magic dust, it always works on the night.'
[Becky Fooks]

Managing rehearsals is the responsibility of the Director. If you already have a Director with a track record to call on to direct your panto, you can skip this next bit. If not, please read on.

Perhaps you are looking for a Director, or you think that you might be that person. What is this animal? He/she needs the organisational skills of the CEO of a multi-national company, the calm of Buddha, the patience of a saint, and have the ability to entertain the masses. He/she needs to be a guide, a mentor, a therapist. He/she must never be short of ideas, or show they doubt that they know the way to get where everyone needs to be. Failing all that he/she must be willing to give all the time and all the energy they are capable of giving for the good of the cause. An unrelenting drive to get the show on the road! If you have such an animal, you have what you need. If you are such an animal, let me shake you by the hand.

Photo: Rehearsing the 'Big Finish' to The Grand Old Duke of York.

More than anything your panto needs someone who is happy to do the job, someone your cast is happy to put their trust in. The cast are not actors. Many would run for the hills if you expected them to 'act'. They are in the cast for many reasons, but acting is not often one of them. Having fun. Joining in. Being with friends. Letting their hair down. These are all very good, genuine reasons. But your cast members are not here to act. So the Director's task is to encourage the cast to pretend, to play, to have a giggle, to be loud, to be big and bold, to be confident about what they are being asked to do. If they are happy on stage, if they are clearly having a good time, the audience will warm to them and the show will go brilliantly. So building confidence in the cast is the number one task for your Director.

Aside Thirteen – A word about preparing the rehearsal space

Let us assume that you are going to rehearse in the space where you will perform the panto in due course. On rehearsal night try and get in early and arrange the space to suit your goal for the evening. I see a priority is to create a suggestion of what it is going to look like at performance, by…

- making sure the performance area, the exits and entrances are all clear.

- putting out any props and set (which might be dummies, as the real props and set are not yet available). So if there is a 'cottage' on stage, use a screen of chairs to suggest it. Anything that helps the cast visualise what is in your head.

- putting out a few rows of chairs to give an idea of where audience will be. This will also help fix where aisles will be. These aisles are often used for entrances and exits as not all characters will come on or go off 'on stage'.

Let me now paint a picture. You schedule an evening of rehearsals beginning at 7.00pm. Some will arrive early. Most will arrive in time. If your community is anything like ours, the cast will immediately want to catch up on Life, the Universe and Everything. In short, they will natter. Some of the topics will be panto related. "How is your costume going?" is a favourite. Some of the youngest might like to run and have a bit of a chase. In simple terms, they are socialising. Now the Director needs to be prepared for this. It will happen. But he/she has a rehearsal that needs to start. What is the strategy? This is where the rows of chairs come in. A brief request is made (maybe with good theatrical volume!) "OK, everyone, please come and sit as we are going to start." The children, with years of school training under their belts, will easily be the first to comply. Some will race to grab what they consider the best seats, ones next to best friends. It is the adults who find it hardest to bring their chit-chat to a conclusion. Some will plead deafness, of course. "Sorry, didn't hear," they say when the request is repeated. But quite quickly the socialising will be under control. The rows of chairs act as a simple way to get everyone's attention. They come. They sit. They face the Director. They are ready... These rows of chairs also act as a 'holding pen' for characters not yet needed in the scene that is about to start. And having people sitting and watching gives cast members on stage a taste of what it is like to have an audience. And if there is feedback from these watchers – smiles, laughter, boos, groans, 'Behind Yous' – it all helps to build the performance on stage.

Aside Fourteen – Basics

Before any rehearsal the Director needs to have planned the basics with military precision (or at least that is what I think I do). Of chief importance are the following:

- knowing where every character is going to enter and exit.

- plotting major moves which result in 'making pictures' on stage.

- having a clear idea of characterisation and able to have a way to get it across, eg: telling the Dame to be like Les Dawson in drag, or telling The Three Little Pigs to be like untalented, wannabe stars off 'The X Factor'.

- being prepared to give an interpretation of what is wanted. Cast need to see what the Director means as well as hear it. For many seeing the Director doing 'it' truly leads to believing that they can do 'it', too.

If, by the end of a rehearsal, your cast have got to grips with these basic points, significant progress has been made. The Director can encourage cast to make notes on their scripts to help them remember. Real actors do, but most panto cast members don't. Young children are blessed with memories that work well (even if not all of them use them). It is the adults who frequently forget or don't even realise that they ever knew a direction... Patience! The Director should never feel that once a scene has been plotted and gone through, he/she won't have to do it all again (from scratch).

Aside Fifteen – And so the rehearsal starts

> 'The rehearsals themselves, in the chilly village hall, always saw a variety of slippers, thermal flasks and, quite often in my case, a heap of last minute homework.'
> [Rosie Marshall]

Nobody has any idea what is in the Director's head and they are waiting to be told and shown. Our 'actors' are not professionals who have already prepared a level of performance, who have a concept as to what motivates their character. Many people with busy lives will come to the first rehearsal of a scene having given the script only a glance. If that. Never forget: Panto might be filling every moment of the Director's waking life (sad, or what?), but the cast have lives they are living with all its trials, tribulations and things they have to plan and make happen. At a rehearsal they simply want to be told and shown what to do. The panto is not another one of life's tasks to worry about. It is about having 'a good time'. The Director is there to do all the spadework. The cast are very happy to be moulded. There will be one or two with their own ideas, who have a natural flair. But that is not the majority.

Act Four – Scene Three: How to get a performance and a few basic bits of stagecraft or 'business'

For many first-time panto performers the stage is a foreign country. Indeed they feel it is so alien that they have no idea what rules apply and how to 'be'. They need to realise that Pantoworld is the real world but in a highly exaggerated form. Its characters are 2-dimensional caricatures but with real feelings. Their feelings and the way they behave are just taken to the extreme. They experience or cause others to experience love, loss, happiness, sadness, fear, and more. It is just that these experiences are made LARGE! A character in love clutches his heart, jumps about, is lit with a pink spotlight (if you have one) and is accompanied by some schmaltzy music. We have come to favour 'Sweet Mystery Of Life' sung by Jeanette MacDonald and Nelson Eddy as our love theme! Another character, who is sad, will bawl their eyes out and produce a giant handkerchief which they then wring out. And yet another character, who is scared, might... Well, let us see. Imagine that Snow White is happily picking flowers in the forest when up creeps The Big Bad Wolf. Of course, there will be a lot of extended 'behind you' business with the audience, before Snow White finally turns to see The Big Bad Wolf in all his scariness.

What does she do? First she does a double take. Nobody in real life would do that. What is it? You know? Good. You don't know? Well, it is something entirely visual and therefore hard to explain in words, but I'll give it a go. Snow White turns slowly and sees the Wolf. She then turns back at normal speed to face the audience. There is a moment for the penny to drop. She turns back more quickly than before to confirm that the Wolf is there...and reacts! Now she could do any of the following:

- scream deafeningly loudly, jump, and run away.

- faint on the spot very, very suddenly.

- faint, but collapse only after a very, very long build-up in which she finally clears the floor where she is to end up, and collapses followed by as many twitches as she fancies.

- thwack the Wolf very hard with her basket of flowers and stroll off like a nice young lady.

Whatever she does, it is extreme. A real reaction, but OTT.

> 'It's just really fun, I guess. Everyone, even people you think you'd never see acting...acting! It's kind of quite cool. When I'm on stage I don't see it as hell. I see it as heaven, really! It's kind of a plus if you like going over the top. It means that you're not really afraid. It's kind of like a competition. See who can go over the top the most.'
> [Emily Russ]

Photo: Going OTT.

Some members of cast take to going over the top like a duck to water. They are what we might call 'naturals'. They are completely at home on stage. They love pretending and showing off. They love to get an audience going. In short, they are in a very, very happy place. Let me give you two real-life examples of 'naturals' from former casts. Of course, our recent casts have been full of 'naturals', too, but we don't want them getting too big for their boots by being told that they are, do we?

So, here are those two examples, Hilary Baker and Alex Gibbons. We've met them both earlier. They are two very different people and had two very different approaches to performing.

Hilary loved being on stage as long as she didn't look anything like her normal self. For her getting the costume right was key. We've read what she has to say about costumes earlier. She loved the disguise. It gave her confidence. It gave her the freedom to enjoy the excessive mischief that the character she was playing could get up to. She set about the task of learning her lines with meticulous care, as she wanted every word to be right and worked hard to do just that. She was always one of the first to know her part and set the benchmark for others – not that she thought that way. Finally, when it came to performance she was always 'in the part'. She had the happy knack of knowing how to do it. She occupied the stage with seeming ease. In short, she was a real actress able to play a range of different types. And the audience loved her. When she was a Goodie she exuded genuine warmth. When she was a Baddie she relished the extreme naughtiness that she could get up to. It wasn't her, Hilary; it was the character.

Photo: Costumes as disguise.

> 'I just love learning the lines! Love it! I go through it loads of times. I just love it. I never `ad that trouble at all. I did it with a tape recorder. I would learn all my lines, put the other lines on the tape - whoever the person was - and just go through it like it was actually happening. I could know it word for word. I could see the page in front of me. I was so exact.'
> [Hilary Baker]

Alex also loved being on stage. He first appeared in 'The Princess and The Dragon' in 2002, aged 10, and he was immediately in his element.

Photo: Young actors in their element.

He was no 'actor'; he was an entertainer. Being on stage was an extension of his real self – the 'cheeky chappie', with a funny comment for every situation. Being on stage that was what was wanted. But Alex was always Alex. The characters he played were him, or versions of him. And like Hilary, the audience loved him. Over the years he appeared in four pantos and when he walked on stage the audience came to know that they were in for some fun. But never expect him to say the lines as written. Learning them was not his strength. I'm not too sure he ever really bothered. He expected it to happen, and if it didn't... no problem. He had total confidence in his ability to wing it. This could make it hard on anyone in scenes with him, but that was not something Alex worried too much about.

That is how I saw Alex, but what does he say of himself?

> 'I was loud and over the top. Possibly acting is learning the script. I was always me in a different costume. Did I learn lines? Yeah. Honestly. It did happen. Not very frequently. I'd read through the words. But if they don't stick... I can remember my special learning script sessions at the Chapel with rope marking the stage. In 'The Grand Old Duke of York' in 2011 I swung onto the stage as the Spider and spoke in Shakespearean verse. That was the bit I enjoyed most of all – the swinging. You told me he's a Shakespearean Spider; go for it. And left it to me.'
> [Alex Gibbons]

It worked brilliantly, and it showed I had learned my lesson!

Photo: The Spider rehearses with Miss Muffet.

His costume, made by Hilary, was one to remember. It has lived on and appeared more than once on New Year's Eve in Bridport.

For much more on costumes go to pages 82-84, 127-130, 148-152.

Both Hilary and Alex were totally at home on stage. Others are, too, to a greater or lesser extent. But many aren't and need to be guided towards a stage performance.

> 'Some of us had never been on a stage before yet Andrew coaxed, cajoled and cudgelled the extrovert out of us, and you could see the faces change from "oh blimey" through

"hey I might just have the hang of this" to, by the end, "bring on the performances!" '
[Dave Crane]

Moving on stage

Major moves need to be choreographed in support of the storyline that is developing. This is known as 'blocking' and results in the making of 'stage pictures'. But crossing a stage can be nerve-wracking for the novice actor. It draws unwanted attention to a person. People are watching! All cast members are able to walk and move in a very convincing fashion – when they are not on stage. But once there many of them lose this lifelong skill. Movement becomes stilted. Arms stop swinging convincingly. People take very strange routes. They move as if they are poorly programmed robots. Sorry, but it is true. This needs to be addressed.

Then, when they have reached where they are meant to be, they become statues. The Director has told X to come on and go to a certain spot. X enters, moves there and promptly becomes rooted. It is as if that spot has immediately become 'home', the only safe place on stage. Then, if X is encouraged to move from it a little when they say a certain line, he/she is quite likely to do the following. One foot remains 'at home' whilst the other takes a tentative step. The line is said and immediately the foot that has moved returns 'home' to join its partner, which has never moved. Cast have no idea they are doing it. They need to be told and then encouraged to 'boldly go' [for all Star Trek fans out there] – to take two steps and occupy this new spot, from which they will move in due course. Lack of movement in a performer is often linked to insecurity on stage and a desire not to draw attention to themselves. Telling someone who is reluctant to move, that a total lack of movement actually attracts attention can convince the most static person to get moving.

Another habit which many cast members demonstrate from time to time is 'reversing'. Instead of turning round to go upstage (= to the back of the stage) they engage reverse and try to back there. It is as if they dare not turn their backs on the audience, even for a second. Of course this habit might be an extreme reaction to the Director telling them not to say their lines upstage. He/she has gone on about not acting with their backs facing the audience. So, yes, maybe the Director is fundamentally to blame for any reversing. Again this is something that needs to be eliminated.

Next there is the problem with 'screening' – when a cast member moves and ends up standing directly in front of another one from the audience's point of view. If, of course, the screening is fleeting, this isn't a problem. If it is longer, the cast member who is out of sight (= the upstage one) has a decision to make. Do they stay out of sight (which some actually want to do) or do they move into view? They should move decisively into view. Not a lean or a shuffle, but a step or two or even more. This resultant move adds another degree of visual interest.

Some cast members will even create screens for themselves. They will intentionally put themselves behind others on stage, or if that isn't possible lurk close to the wings, where they are out of sight for a good section of the audience. On stage there is no hiding place allowed! [Unless it serves the plot.]

Finally, when it comes to movement and the stage picture, there is 'the line up'. This is where your cast members on stage end up standing in a straight line across the stage, usually with very equal spaces between them all. Is this the demonstration of some sort of Universal Law? One that states: 'Put any number of people on stage and they will achieve a straight line with equidistant spacings'. I think it might be, because everyone does it, and some find it hard not to do it even when it is pointed out. They can be told to re-arrange themselves more interestingly, and they do so quite easily. But before you know it, the line has re-emerged. Time needs to be spent on demonstrating the 'Art of Grouping'. This means having people stand with different spacings between them, not all facing the same way, with some a little more upstage than others. When in doubt, create curves and/or sub groups.

And what about the little-known skill of 'huddling', which is very useful on small stages?

> 'Trying to fit the entire cast onto the stage in any particular scene usually resulted in the instruction to 'huddle'. The looming edge of the stage with the dwarves in 'Robin Hood' called for a 'catcher'. This element of teamwork and looking after each other is something Charlotte recalls in one of the earlier shows where she'd said, "I can't huddle anymore", and Robert, in true panto spirit, replied, "Oh, but we can."'
> [Rosie Marshall]

The Skill of 'Watching'

Photo: The cast of 'Mother Hubbard' watching and huddling.

This is a basic requirement for the creation of a dynamic 'stage picture'. By it I mean that everyone on stage needs to be involved in the action, even if they have no lines whatsoever. 'Watching' is the answer; watching what is going on. Watching means that they are also listening to what's going on (and it helps them pick up on cues). They are fulfilling the role of an onstage audience. Doing so helps the actual audience sitting out front to focus. Watching is a fundamental requirement of crowds in crowd scenes. It is a truth to say that if you have a single cast member not watching, much like the static cast member talked about above, he or she will act as an audience magnet and be watched in turn by them.

Lines

We have talked of 'straight lines' above. Now we must address the thorny issue of learning lines. There is no panto without them. Unless you are aiming for a radical, all-improvised production, there are lines to be learned. Everybody will have some lines – anything from one to very many. At some point the

Director will want them to be learned. As we've seen there will of course be some people who will hope to wing it, and might be very skilled at doing just that. The Director might prefer they didn't do that, and may battle hard to get them to learn them. One or two people will never fully learn them and not worry themselves too much about it. They know the gist, and they adlib.

Most of the cast, however, will want to know their lines as written. They won't feel confident without them well known before the curtain goes up.

[More about adlibbing on pages 146-148.]

So how are lines learned?

This advice is from children.

> 'I learned them with my Mum. I read them to her and she did all the other lines.'
> [Matthew Medley]

> 'I don't really learn them. I just remember them.'
> [William Fooks]

Many children appear to learn lines by osmosis. They haven't lost the ability to learn because they are doing it all the time. It's as natural as breathing to them. They read the script; the scene is rehearsed; the lines are as good as learned.

And if you hit a problem learning lines, what should you do?

> 'You just try and remember, and if you don't remember, just make different ones.'
> [Jack House]

That couldn't be simpler, could it?

And, finally, a blunt message.

> 'Just keep going as if you know your lines, `cos that's the only way you're gonna survive.'
> [Emily Russ]

Many adult cast members find the whole lines-learning process harder. Some of them find it far harder. They don't all love learning lines – not like Hilary Baker for whom it was a pleasure as we've seen above. For some it can become a trial. What have they got to say?

'A good male toilet has adequate reading material and sometimes the best reading material is a script. Because that's a time when you can sit quietly and not be interrupted and talk to yourself.'
[John Horne]

'I've found what helps is if you know where you are in the scene and say something then regardless of the person before you.'
[Alan Clark]

'It takes me hours and hours of repetition until the dog thinks I've gone mad.'
[Brian Hesketh]

How can line-learners be helped? There are a number of ways. Different ways work for different people, but all involve an investment of time and effort. It is true that most people find lines easier to learn once a scene has been plotted or set on stage. As they learn their lines they can visualise where they are going to say them and where the characters are to whom they are going to say them. Do you see?

Advice to the Line Learner

Work methodically down a section of script a few lines at a time. Read your lines, cover them, try to repeat them, check. And only when these few lines are fixed, move on to the next few lines. As you go do not skip the lines that are not yours. They need to be read each time, too. This helps you learn your cues. Repeat the process with the next section. Then, before moving on to anything new, return to where you started and go from there. This means that you are 'stitching' the lines together in your head. This also means that the repetition gets longer as more learned lines are added. Stop at the end of a page. Have a rest. Go back to it and see how well you can do. You only move on to the next section of lines to be learned, when you've got the first lines well bedded in. Don't panic. The rehearsal period gives you time as long as you start the process of line learning early.

In addition:

- Get help from a parent, partner or friend to sit with you and run your lines a bit at a time. You need someone patient.

- Make an audio recording of the lines you don't say, leaving gaps for you to put in your lines.

- Transfer the script on to a digital gadget, so that it can travel anywhere and be looked at anywhere, anytime.

Never forget that cues are as important as lines, because if the cast don't give the right cues they make life very hard for the characters they are on stage with.

Even people who have a track record for not learning their lines can surprise.

> 'In one panto John and I not only learned our own lines (yes, what a shock!) but also knew each other's, with the result that I once prompted him only for him to loudly tell the audience: "No, there's no need to prompt me, I have learned my lines and my next line is…" and so on.'
> [Dave Crane]

A truth:

The Director must be aware that some people who have performed for many years find that they begin to doubt their ability to learn lines as they get older. It is a great shame when a former star stops performing because of this loss of confidence. Would they be happy doing a smaller part, perhaps the chance of having a scene-stealing role?

> 'I was getting older – I'm 75 – and I stopped because I didn't want to be that "silly old fool" on the stage.'
> [Mary Trott]

But former stage performers can and do continue to participate in pantos in any number of off-stage roles.

The mention of scene-stealing roles has reminded me of something – my own fondness for a role where an impact can be made but with little or no responsibility for the panto as a whole. So let us meet...

The Director as Frustrated Actor

I have enjoyed being on stage in front of an audience for as long as I can remember. I am sometimes surprised that everyone doesn't get the same pleasure from it, or feel at home there. As a result, over the years, I have awarded myself a kind of perk in some of our pantos – giving myself a small scene-stealing role.

Occasionally during the process of writing a panto an idea has popped into my head and a character has appeared – one, which I fancy doing myself. The undercover policeman in 'Aladdin and the Princesses' is a case in point. How could I not want to play the part? After all, his disguise was that of a Giant Parrot! But how could that be? The character had this to explain to a bemused Aladdin and his small sidekick, Halfpint.

📷 Photo: The Director as Parrot with Halfpint.

> *Halfpint:*
>   *But you're a... a... a...*
> *Parrot:*
>   *I believe the word you are looking for is 'Parrot'. The*

>   *hooked beak and brilliant plumage are a bit of a giveaway, aren't they?*
>
> Halfpint:
> >   *But you... you...you...*
>
> Parrot:
> >   *Talk? [Halfpint nods.] Fluently. Cantonese. Pekinese. Knocked-knees. Any 'nese' you can name.*
>
> Aladdin:
> >   *I had a parrot for five years, but he never said a word.*
>
> Halfpint:
> >   *How come?*
>
> Aladdin:
> >   *He was stuffed.*
>
> Parrot:
> >   *Oh, very droll.*
>
> Aladdin:
> >   *What are you doing here?*
>
> Parrot:
> >   *[checks all is clear] Shhh! I am a member of the Peking Anti-Pirate Undercover Parrot Patrol. PAPUPP for short. I am not in fact a real parrot. This is, believe it or not, a disguise! I can see you are surprised. You're probably asking yourselves, "Why a parrot?" Well pirates and parrots are very close. Sometimes too close. But that's another matter. As long as I say "Pieces of Eight" every now and then and moult every six months, they suspect nothing...*

[And between them Aladdin, Halfpint and the Parrot come up with a plan to retrieve the Princesses who have been captured by the Pirates.]

It's only now that I realise how many talking animals we've had in our pantos, and how the fact that they talk is often hard for other characters to come to terms with.

Getting to be the Giant Parrot in one of Sue Dodge's brilliant costumes was a definite highlight for the frustrated actor – for the director who would quite fancy playing all the parts given the chance!

Aside Sixteen – Prompter?

If you decide to have a prompter – a person sitting off stage with a script ready to offer lines to cast members during the show if/when they grind to a halt, – he/she needs to attend rehearsals on a regular basis throughout the rehearsal period. They then become familiar with the flow; they know when a silence is a theatrical pause or a piece of 'business' and not forgotten lines; they learn the idiosyncrasies of the cast and the way they perform. Unless you have a prompter able and willing to commit to the long haul, don't contemplate having one. The skills you require in a prompter are boldness and volume. A hesitant and/or inaudible prompt is less use than no prompt at all.

Pace

Panto needs to be a romp – both in the fun sense and in the speed sense. It is not a reflective thing. It moves on at pace, a roller coaster ride. Keeping the pace up can be hard. During the early phase of the rehearsal period when the cast have scripts in their hands pace can be built up and maintained. The performance is yet to come, but things can move quickly because the cast are not worrying about what to say next. Then the first brave souls put their scripts down (or shove them in their back pockets) and have a go from memory. Of course it is to be expected that the pace of the scene will slow. Memory can take time to unearth the next line. An actor can be slow to realise that a cue has just been given. This is an unavoidable phase and the Director needs to be understanding. Stepping into a scene on stage without a copy of the script in hand is a nerve-wracking thing for almost everyone and they need every encouragement.

A tendency at this time is for the actors, struggling to remember what they should say, to give reworked or re-imagined versions of their lines instead of the actual, or close to actual, ones. This should only be acceptable for a short while. If it is not brought to their attention and dealt with, the actors will be re-inventing their lines every time they say them. It is one thing to 're-write' and then always deliver this re-worked version, as consistency is what everyone wants. It is quite another to be generating a new variation of the line(s) on each and every occasion.

Why isn't this a good thing? The constant re-working means constant thinking and silent re-writing by the actor. This makes for slower delivery and frequently makes the storyline less clear and so harder for the audience to follow. If the actor is alone on stage, that is his/her problem. But if he/she is in a scene with others, it is unfair on them if he/she never gives consistent cues.

Also, if the writer is present he/she might get peeved at having the lines they have crafted and slaved over for weeks treated in such a cavalier fashion!

The right pace is only achieved once all the cast have their lines learned and have achieved consistency. Then the show can romp along as it should.

Be aware that pace does not mean 'go as fast as is humanly possible'. Pace does not mean rushing lines – instead it means picking up on cues and only having pauses where they serve the storyline in some way. Teenagers, especially, can be prone to speaking so fast that they move at a speed that older listeners call 'gabbling'. They need to realise that older ears need slower speech. The cast needs also to realise that pace will be affected by the presence of an audience. This is something to be borne in mind throughout Act Five: Scene One – 'Working the Audience', pages 138-148.

At last the time comes to put the script down and trust to memory.

> 'There was a kind of honeymoon period when, once we'd run through and fixed the entrances, moves and exits, scripts were just about tolerated... but then came the dreaded edict "no scripts on stage". Aargh! But somehow it all worked out OK, and Andrew did say that if I really had to adlib, just make sure a) you remember the cueing line at the end and b) do it before the audience start heading for the exit.'
> [Dave Crane]

Volume

📷 Photo: Young soldiers wanting to be heard.

> 'She knows all the other lines. She's got a brilliant memory. It's just volume! I know she knows the lines. It's just can anyone hear her say them?'
> [Becky Fooks talking about daughter, Ellie.]

Once the lines are learned they need to be audible. There is nothing more frustrating than hearing members of the audience at the end of a show saying how much they enjoyed it, but it was a shame they couldn't hear so-and-so. All the cast need to be encouraged to project, to talk to the back row of seats. If characters are standing next to each other, they still need to speak at volume as if the whole width of the stage was between them. Too often they are prone to slipping into 'natural volume' and start to become inaudible beyond the first few rows.

Stage microphones help if you have them. We have three of them hanging from above the stage. But people still need to pump out the volume. Radio mikes would be a boon, but we've never had them. Children with their smaller voices are often the least able to project. We've all heard them shouting. We know they are capable of volume. But they find it physically tiring to maintain it. And the naturally quiet or shy ones find it a real challenge.

Parents can come up with their own strategy to make sure their children can be heard.

> 'Learning the lines was difficult. My Mum and Dad would sit at the kitchen table and I'd stand at the end of the hallway and say my lines and they'd see if they could hear me.'
> [Emily Chubb]

Act Four – Scene Four: Children on stage – How to get them to give of their best (and adults too!)

As the subject of child performers has come up more than once already, let us address it now. First let's deal with a contemporary worry head on – the relationships of adults with children. We have all read the horror stories. I'm sure you know what I'm referring to. How do we proceed?

We do not seek CRB/DBS clearance, nor do we expect anyone to do so. These are checks made into the background of people working with children and vulnerable groups with a view to discovering any criminal history that would bar people from doing such work. Instead we expect parents to be responsible for their children and make decisions accordingly. If a young child has not been in a panto cast before, we want one of their parents to be present during the rehearsals until both the parents and the child are happy. They then can choose to attend rehearsals or not. It is up to them. However, there are always three or more parents who attend any rehearsal. We also have parents and their children in the panto cast together. And we have two Production Assistants whose role includes supervising the children. Keeping an eye on them. Establishing a home base for them to return to between scenes. Keeping any excesses of energy in check. These P.A.s for the last few pantos have been a retired teacher and a registered childminder. As the Director I cannot thank them enough. They enable the children to be confident, to enjoy what they're doing and so give great performances.

As the panto is a whole community venture the presence of all ages is a given. It is less and less common these days for all ages to work together to a common goal, to achieve something as a group. For us it is central that we come together and work co-operatively to create something everyone can be proud to be a part of.

How do we keep children motivated throughout the rehearsal period?

Like everyone they want to have a good time. They have spent days at school, and rehearsals should not be an extension of their experience there. Panto is different. They have chosen to do it and once on board they owe it their commitment. But they don't have to do it – nobody does. Yet, they do have to give it their best shot and the Director must have the highest expectations of them. Oh, and like everyone in the cast they have to have FUN!

Let's look at them in two age groups – those at primary school and then those of secondary school age.

Photo: Snow White with all 14 Dwarfs.

Children aged up to 11 are best engaged if they are given the freedom to indulge their delight in cheek and naughtiness. Controlled cheek and naughtiness. Cheek and naughtiness that are harnessed for the good of the production. Even the quietest children like to have permission to let rip and be silly. It might take them a little while to realise that what you are asking them to do is not only allowed, but is being encouraged. Over the years we have come to realise that if they are given this opportunity at the outset, they are instantly won over and are then happy to apply themselves to the 'quieter' stuff in due course.

Here is an example from the 2013 panto, 'Robin Hood', which is still fresh in my mind. The team of children, all 14 of them, aged 4 to 10, were Dwarfs. Not the traditional 7, but 14. They were divided into two groups of 7, each with a 10-year-old as leader. The first thing they were invited to do in the very first rehearsal was the following: All were to shout a couple of lines very loudly together from a long way off. Then, in two teams, they were to run in single file down two aisles through the auditorium to the stage. On arrival the last to arrive in each line bumped into the one in front and like dominoes all of them fell over. This entrance appealed to them greatly. They couldn't believe their luck – shouting, running and falling over in the very first minute - and they wanted to rehearse it again, immediately! When they then realised that within a few lines of dialogue they were all to do a double take, 'see' the audience, scream with 'fear' and run and hide we knew we had them! None of them had that worried look that children on stage can often have. They knew they were in a great place. Their faces showed it. And they were hotwired for whatever was coming next.

How can we keep these young children feeling enthusiastic over the weeks of rehearsal? Some guidelines that have worked for us.

- Tell them they are good, but ask them if they believe they can be better. Because you think they could be.

- Having praised them, 'raise the bar' by introducing something new for them to do in a scene that they know well. Always have something new up your sleeve. A new bit of business. New moves. A new line or two, maybe. Asking them if they'd like to do something extra will always get a positive response from some (or even all).

- Have challenges for them. "Who can say their line loud enough to be heard outside the rehearsal space?" "Who can sing something that needs singing?" "Who can belch at the mention of food?" (Boys love this!])

- Give them the chance to offer ideas, eg: "The panto's missing something. Can you help? I need a joke about X, does anyone know a good one?"

- Encourage them to give feedback about the scene they are doing.

- Giving a special thing to do to a quiet child, a child with poor concentration or one with energy to burn, a special thing, which only they are going to do, works well if thought has gone into what you ask them to do. They feel special as a result. The following has worked well: Three small, quiet, seemingly angelic girls were given the chance to chase three adult Baddies with dummy axes! A highly energetic lad was asked if he could sneak up on a character (who incidentally was being played by his father in real life) and jump on him and ride him like a horse! [See 'best bits' below.] For all four children their moments in the spotlight were high points of the show.

- Give different people responsibility for different elements. One to lead an exit. Another to organise the group before they come on. Another to start the singing. And so on.

What do young children recall as being 'best bits'?

'The big chases, where you get to run.'
[Amy House]

'Running! Jumping on Dad was the best, best, best, best, best part!!! And going "yee-har!"
[Jack House, the energetic lad mentioned above.]

'In the Chase. You were one of the guards. I ran between your legs. We had to run round the Hall. And I liked it when we were watching it.'
[William Fooks, talking to his father.]

'The Chase. The big one. Me and Isabel had axes. We chased two of the guards.'
[Ellie Fooks]

'I liked getting to know new people and getting to work with other people.'
[Grace Bellorini]

'The best bit about being a dwarf was I got lifted up at one point and showed to the audience.'
[Rosa Bellorini]

What do their parents say?

'It's fantastic. We really, really missed it when it'd finished. It's a lot of rehearsals, but there was not one single time when they didn't look forward to it. They were raring to get there. And they got such a lot out of it. They were both very shy the first time we took them along. But that just passed. And they found their confidence.'
[Jenny Bellorini]

Building confidence is an oft-reported bonus from being on stage in a panto.

> 'I love the effect it has on them. Their confidence grows. The way they mix with the other children in the village, and the adults in the village. They look forward to the rehearsals. They love it. And it's brilliant watching them do it. Ellie's face particularly, beams! Whenever she's on stage - a massive big grin. And the way the older kids and adults look after the littler kids. A really good opportunity for them.'
> [Becky Fooks]

And building confidence is not just for the youngest children in the casts.

> 'Since doing the panto I've done a lot more public speaking than I used to at school. And I quite enjoy doing it. But I probably enjoy panto more than public speaking just because you've got a character. In public speaking you are just yourself. Panto is a lot less scary.'
> [James Russ]

📷 Photo: Snow White, Robin Hood, Maid Marian, Little John, Red Riding Hood, and Wilma Scarlet.

Children aged 11+ want to be seen and treated as individuals, especially as they get older. By their mid-teens they have often experienced being in more than one previous panto and have learned a great deal about being on stage. As a result they definitely have ideas as to how scenes could be played and should be invited to offer them. But they do not know everything! They may be naturals on stage, but need to be given a clear framework within which to act and give of their best. The Director needs to be ready with explanations. How can we keep them happy and enthused?

📷 Photo: What!

Many of them love to carry as much of the storyline as the panto can give them.

'I'm not me when I'm acting. I am an artist! I become the character! I'm not Lottie any more when I step on that stage. I'm Dribbler or Desdemona or Maid Marian. I really enjoyed her. I should've got an Oscar for that! I think all my characters are aggressive people! I'm so shy as normal but I let it all out. Ella owns the stage. Apart from when I'm on it with her. Because, then I own it!'
[Lottie Hyde]

- They are able to learn a great deal of script (often much more than the adults) and this talent should be harnessed.

- They respond well to responsibility and the recognition that their characters are major players and that their performances are important.

  'I enjoyed playing Martha Muffet because I had a bigger part then! But YOU adlibbed for ages and then forgot your next line in MY scene.'
  [Ella Horne telling her father off.]

- Encourage them to work with their ideas and then review how it went. They can be very self-aware and quickly learn what works and what doesn't. They often spark ideas off each other.

- Though they may show some signs of reserve at the start of the rehearsal period – as they may not know each other well – once they get inside their panto characters they soon relax.

  'As a process I recall the thought of having to go to a rehearsal quite a drag, but by the time we walked to the Village Hall and began our scenes, it was such a laugh.'
  [Zacyntha Dunhill]

- Never underestimate the social side of the whole panto process. Teenagers may seem to communicate only via digital devices these days, but they thrive on real-life. Panto can offer that reality!

- They are still children at heart and still love the chance to be silly or anarchic or preferably, both. Give them the chance to be so. Being a teenager is not necessarily easy. Panto offers the chance to exist in a parallel universe, a 'place' where the pressures of presenting the right style/image/fashion, etc simply don't come into play. Even the 'cool' ones can shake off the shackles of coolness, and often seem to relish the happy release when the pressure to maintain cool is lifted.

'You go into the process knowing it's going to be silly. There's no way you're ever gonna be the cool one in the pantomime. `Cos in reality no one is the cool one in the pantomime. Ever. They're all complete idiots!'
[Emily Russ]

- Girls especially need to be happy in what their characters are going to look like and wear. Bear this in mind in order to get them to give of the best. Teenage girls can lose the self-confidence they had as younger children and roles need to be given to them in which they feel comfortable.

'Speaking of costumes, they were always a cause of much anticipation as the weeks of rehearsals progressed. Rosemary would produce various brightly coloured pieces of material and measuring tapes until she eventually appeared with a complete dress or ensemble, which could only be acceptable in panto-land! Charlotte, who has always been adamant that she does not wear pink, insists that she was, not once, but twice forced into a pink (peach!) dress. Her worry for her 'girly' reputation was unnecessary when the audience experienced her singing, and the rest of the cast her breaking of a feather duster.'
[Rosie and Charlotte Marshall]

- The teenage boys in your cast can possibly feel that the stage is a 'girly' place, or a place just for young children. But...

'I went through a phase of thinking before the first one. "No, Really not! Don't get involved in that" But after the

first one I found out I quite like making people laugh. And people did actually laugh. Not just at the words but at the actions as well.'
[James Russ]

- The more opportunities for 'action' that teenage performers are given, the better. Giving them interesting and/or complicated bits of physical business to do challenges them to raise their game. And, don't overlook the fact that they are usually the fittest people in your cast, as well as being the quickest to catch on. So if you can give them the chance to swing on a rope, to hide in boxes, to leap and jump and throw themselves about, do so. Pantos are definitely not only about 'the words' – (even though the writer may sometimes think otherwise) – and every opportunity for physical fun cranks up the level of a performance.

- Also never overlook the other talents teenage children might have that can be incorporated within the panto. Can they juggle or stiltwalk or turn somersaults? Just think what they could add to a panto. We have had children singing alone or in groups, dancing, making music on piano and flute. It is fair to say that these have all been girls, all of whom have enjoyed the recognition of their skills. You can find that a teenager who sings is happy to lead a 'choir' of younger children.

- For the teenage boys in your cast the adult 'blokes' are a bonus. By their presence they provide a role model, and give the stamp of approval to the enterprise. If these blokes are up for making fools of themselves, being truly silly in character, it must be OK to do likewise. When, let us say, one of the blokes playing an incompetent Guard adopts a loud 'mummerset' accent and gurns and goes way OTT, the jaws of many children drop. It is as if a film has been lifted from their eyes. Behind their growing grins they are saying: "Wow! Is this what panto is about? I want some of it!"

In your cast should children be Goodies or Baddies? Does it matter? We have had children as both. But whether they are one or the other, they are always children or age-less. We never want them pretending to be grown-ups; even the older teenage children. As Baddies or as Goodies their characters are always funny, silly, cheeky, clever, feisty, raucous, energetic, brave, sometimes heroic and always fond of very bad jokes – but not usually all at the same time. The only difference is that as Baddies they will be on the losing side. 'Oh, yes, they will!' After all, this is panto.

Over the years children have been Thieves, Witches, Nursery Rhyme Characters, Trolls, Gnomes, Pirates, Soldiers, Guards, Fairies, Princesses, Sheep, Rats, Dwarfs and the children of The Old Woman Who Lived In A Shoe, among others. You can decide whether they were being Goodies or Baddies at the time.

As we have seen, teenagers have also been called upon to play some of the above, plus secondary leads and, in some cases, leading characters such as Robin Hood, Snow White, Red Riding Hood, Aladdin and Dick Whittington. In leading roles teenagers have warmed to the challenge of playing scenes with adults, especially if it means getting the better of them. Causing the adult characters to look ridiculous is always fun and keeps energy levels up. Having young people set an adult character up for a fall is looked forward to, and the audience enjoys it too.

It is true to say that teenage performers are at the heart of our pantos – driving the plots forward, carrying much of the storyline, offering role models for the younger children to copy, and by the quality of their performances reminding the adults of how high the bar can be!

It needs to be remembered that for children who have grown up performing panto every couple of years, the whole experience is very special. We have heard how playing the Baddie was a life-changing turning point! [See Neuralgia in Act Two: Scene Two, page 35-37.] But that is not all...

> 'Being a part of the Drimpton village pantomime over the years was always a great experience. I feel that having the opportunity from a young age to appear on stage has paved the way for me to continue acting and performing since I left school and went to university, where I have acted in revues and plays, as well as delving into the world of writing, directing and producing (realising that our

Director's increasing levels of stress were completely justified!).'
[Joe Horne, who acted in our pantos from the age of 4 to 18.]

When will Joe direct his first panto? Watch this space. But Joe has been beaten by his sister, Ella, 16, and her friend, Lottie, 17, both Drimpton pantomimers, who, in December 2014, re-introduced panto to their secondary school in the multiple roles of writers/producers/directors and stars!

Ideas on costuming children. Here is what our current Costume Chief has to say.

> 'Costumes need to be cheap and simple when large numbers are involved. This can be achieved in several ways.
>
> - Use a unisex design and something which does not require a great deal of sewing or fitting. T Shirts or tabards are a good base to start with.
>
> - Remnants / Cheap supply of material can be an inspiration.
>
> - Find inspiration from Fancy Dress costume ideas / designs on line.
>
> - Ask parents / guardians to provide trousers, shorts, tights or whatever is required for lower half of body.
>
> - Workshops that get children and adults involved in mass production of accessories are great fun.

Footwear is often a problem. Pumps, plimsolls, daps – whatever they are called in your area – are often the best solution – again provided from home.

Hats / Headgear – If you are lucky you may have someone locally who enjoys hat / mask making if it is not your forte. Our hat makers, have turned cereal packets of all types and sizes into a range of headgear.'
[Rosemary Shepherd]

Involvement of Adults in creation of Costumes and Props

Costume making needs a Team of Helpers:

'It is quite likely that there will be a number of adults who are keen to be involved in the production of a Panto but NOT on stage. It is necessary to get to know these people and their strengths and talents. This is not always easy and one must be prepared for the occasional disasters, which have to be diplomatically rectified.

Costume Workshops are a good way of getting to know people. What needs to be planned?

Have the following available:

- Several sewing machines and operators.

- Cottons, Elastic, pins, needles, scissors etc.
- Ironing Boards and Irons.
- Tea, Coffee, Squash, Biscuits.

Photo: a costume workshop.

Identify tasks. Some are one-offs. Others are mass production:

One-offs: These tasks can be given to known perennial helpers initially. Have all necessary items for the task ready along with simple instructions and if possible a sketch or picture of what it is hoped the final article should look like.

Mass Production: These items will hopefully be basic and straightforward. A production line for a group of volunteers with a team leader can be a good way of using a variety of skills and levels of ability.

Unfinished items can be shared out to be taken home by those who feel confident to do so.

Make sure all volunteers feel valued and leave feeling that they have contributed.'
[Rosemary Shepherd]

Sometimes a costume idea might not come off as intended. But the result may be better than could have been planned. A recent example is the Guards' costumes in 'Robin Hood'. The original plan was to have knitted 'chain mail' and papier-mâché helmets.

'It was like one of these comedy shows when they say "About turn!" and the helmets turned about half-an-hour later. And the knitted chain mail top was fine, apart from the fact it grew! Every time you wore it, it seemed to get narrower. I think the stitches sagged, so instead of being round, they went oblong. Day 1 it was at your knees. Day 2 it was down to your calves. Day 3 it was at your ankles.'
[Alan Clark, one of the Guards.]

Photo: Guards with Lady Thighslapper.

And now, back to the cast. Having looked at ways of getting good performances from children, what about the adults?

Handling adults in the cast

Many, if not all of the earlier guidelines for maintaining enthusiasm levels in children apply to your adult members of cast, too. But they have particular needs. They need to:

- be encouraged to leave normal life at door.

- be given every encouragement to go OTT.

- rediscover the joy of 'play' and 'pretending'.

- have their worries about line-learning dealt with, not glossed over. Give strategies. [Refer back to Act Four: Scene Three – Advice to the Line Learner, page 112.]

- have little or no responsibility for the panto in general.

- be assured that none of them will be made a fool of.

- **HAVE FUN!**

Life can be a serious business and being an adult is a full-time job 24/7. Panto is another world, where such demands can be set aside.

> 'Among people of our age there was a feeling that we're all going to have a play, have a go. It was a great time to leave your hang-ups at the door. "We've gotta concentrate on this, so forget about the rest of it for now." I wasn't feeling great at the time, but it wasn't to do with the panto. And I'm not a natural team player. But I really, really enjoyed it – did me the world of good.'
> [Mark House]

Fun? Yes. But the Director needs to have high expectations. How is the role of 'The Director' seen from the viewpoint of a member of the cast.

Photo: The Grand Old Duke of York (Brian Hesketh) in his grand costume, made by his wife.

'From experience that we've had here or elsewhere I don't think it matters how good a cast you've got, how good a script you've got, if you don't have someone who is willing and able to, at times, – maybe not be unpopular – but to make people bristle and so be good enough to perform – then you're not going to have a good show. You do need that direction – someone who can see what you're doing well. Someone to see how things need tuning, improving, pushing on.

One of the things with the Director is the way in which you get told things that you need to be told, even if you don't think you need to be told. And even if you think you've been told before. And even if you're being told completely the opposite to what you think you were told last time. Oh, yes, he does! We all have enough respect for the Director to know there is an overall vision ticking away at least in one person's head. And it is the Director's job to put that vision in front of the audience. So you grit your teeth and get on with it! Curse him under your breath and mutter about him on the way home.'
[Brian Hesketh]

Act Four – Scene Five: Chases

When is the right time to talk about chases? Is it now? Why not?

> 'Every Drimpton pantomime's highlight was its cast running around the Hall, limbs flailing, bumping into each other and performing general, mostly accidental, acrobatics. I can remember hanging onto my rollers in 'The Grand Old Duke of York' whilst conga-ing through the audience, and Charlotte definitely lost a shoe in one performance careering round a corner.'
> [Rosie Marshall]

Chases of one sort or another lay at the heart of every panto story. We've seen how much they are remembered as being among 'the best bits' for the children in our casts. At some point (and more than once in a panto) Goodies will be doing their best to catch the Baddies, or the Baddies will be trying to catch the Goodies. That is how it is. That is what the audience expects. The Chase can be of various basic types at different speeds and of different lengths involving any number of people.

- round and round the stage.

- round and round a piece of scenery, eg: a giant tree, that is on the stage.

- exiting stage right and re-appearing stage left = going round and round off-stage.

- exiting the stage and entering the auditorium, where the route takes it anywhere the Director wants!

- exiting the auditorium completely and re-entering from somewhere else entirely.

These types can be stitched together in any way you fancy. But a key thing for the cast to learn is the skill of 'comic running'. Children, especially, will see The Chase as a chance to show that they are fast runners and can catch the person they are chasing. But this is panto, not the Olympics. We don't want Usain Bolt, we want Benny Hill. So forget real speed, our chasers need to run funnily! It looks fast, but isn't. Funny running with a continuous adlibbed commentary from all participants in The Chase is what the panto needs. Then factor in opportunities for misdirection, for 'behind yous' and for comic 'skid' turns, where chasers almost lose their footing as they change direction, and The Chase becomes a comic highpoint.

During the best Chase, the tables are turned! The chasers become chased and the other way around. To have the smallest and the youngest character get the better of the biggest and the baddest is a moment that cannot fail but get the audience cheering.

Whatever you do, allow plenty of rehearsal time to getting your chases sharp and slick and safe. Make certain everyone knows who they are chasing and where. And ensure that everyone knows to be careful. In our most recent panto, 'Robin Hood', when, close to the end, the Sheriff of Nottingham (boo! hiss!) brought on his 4 Guards and 4 Lumberjacks to seize Robin, his 4 Merry Men & Maids and Snow White and all her 14 Dwarfs, there was a moment of calm before ALL were involved in The Chase! Yes, all of them. That is 28 people aged from 4 to 70 all chasing or being chased all round our venue – on stage, off-stage, in the auditorium packed with c150 people, and even outside the venue! And, they all survived intact. It looked madly chaotic, but was precisely choreographed. And it was funny, which was the idea.

INTERVAL

Time for another breather. Time to review progress.

And so the weeks pass, and the scenes go into their second or third rehearsal. With luck they are becoming bedded in. Exits and entrances are all sorted. The cast all know what they should be doing and when they should be doing it, even if they need reminding. The Director does his/her best to remain understanding and patient.

A confession:

I am not a saint, and everyone attached to the panto, who has been in one before, knows that at some point my patience will run out. It can happen in an instant and the result is... I shout. Then it is over and we move on. I'm sorry, but that is how it is.

> 'You've always said every time: "I want it to be fun." But there is a time to say: "Stop messing about. This needs to be done. I'm not happy with this. It isn't good enough." You still have to come along bubbling and laughing. With the occasional command which pulls us up a bit. But it needs to be done.'
> [Rod Bracher]

By the midway point of rehearsals, everything has been plotted. Everyone in the cast has done all the bits of the scenes they are in at least once, and in most cases 3 or 4 times (or even more). It is time to hand out the second schedule covering the period up to and including the performance(s). This should take into account whatever scenes are considered to be weak points, and which are in need of more work than others. It is also time for rehearsals to cover longer sections of the panto. Parts of scenes that have been rehearsed in isolation begin to be stitched together. For the first time we begin to see how scenes flow. Later still in the rehearsal period we run a few scenes in order. Step by step we get nearer to running a whole act.

Throughout the total rehearsal period (after the first few sessions) it is possible that groups of characters arrange rehearsals independent of the Director. They are not staging a coup! Far from it. They are showing how much they want to get it right and do their best. They are also showing how much they are enjoying themselves and the social side of putting the panto on. For much of the time we were rehearsing 'Robin Hood', the men playing Lumberjacks – all of whom were new to panto – got together in the house of one of them (which happened to be next door to where I live), with beer and food and had a grand time 'rehearsing'. I know they were, because I could often hear them singing the Monty Python 'Lumberjack Song' through the wall until late at night.

> 'The team of Lumberjacks took it quite seriously! We'd never sung on stage before – if you can call it singing. The four of us managed to get together and have a couple of beers and thoroughly enjoyed several evenings in private rehearsals! There was one occasion when the Lumberjacks tottered off into the forest at about 3.30 in the morning, I think!'
> [Danny Kirk, Lumberjack]

And the trio of women playing The Three Little Pigs regularly got together to run their lines, to go through their dance routine, to sing their song, and to plan their amazing costumes [often, but not always, with the Big Bad Wolf in tow].

I think it is fair to say The Three Little Pigs had a ball from start to finish.

> 'Although the panto is fun, the Pigs and The Wolf really wanted to be as professional as possible, so we organised informal weekly rehearsals at each other's houses in order to gossip, drink tea and the occasional wine, eat cake, look at funny clips on YouTube, and of course practise, practise, practise.'
> [Leigh Carroll-Smith]

Photo: The Three Little Pigs with The Big Bad Wolf.

As for the teenage cast members, they would meet up via Facebook and who knows what they talked about.

... all ages can work together...

ACT FIVE

Including: The Last Ten Days. 'Working the Audience'. One Day To Go! – The Dress Rehearsal.

Act Five – Scene Setting:
The Last Ten Days

> 'I do remember poor Andrew having stern words with us about not remembering our lines (increasingly and more erratically so as the opening night grew closer).'
> [Zacyntha Dunhill]

In the last ten days of a rehearsal period the following rehearsals need to be scheduled in the following order.

- A full run of the first half up to the interval in order with sets and props.

- A full run of the second half from the interval to the end with sets and props.

- A full run of the whole panto with sets and props. Followed by feedback/notes.

- A full run with all the technical stuff – lighting, sound, and rehearsing scenery and set changes. Followed by feedback/notes.

- A dress rehearsal with everything in place – full costume, make-up, lights, sound, sets, props, music. And don't forget to rehearse the bows.

These can be long sessions and need careful planning. The cast needs to be warned that they might be needed for a long time (but in reality anything after 9.30pm is seldom a creative use of time). Clearly the parents of young children are told that they can take their children home as and when if the session is going on. Most parents are willing for their children to have one or two late evenings as long as it's not a school day next day. We also tell all cast to bring something to eat, while we offer free hot drinks or squash.

These final big rehearsals are where the panto really comes together. Of course, if sets and props and maybe any 'difficult' or 'hard to use' costumes have been available to be used for some time before, that's a plus.

Act Five – Scene One 'Working the Audience'

Towards the end of the rehearsal period the subject of 'working the audience' needs to be raised. By this time the cast are very familiar with the script and are generally confident. They now need a few Tips & Wrinkles on how to get the audience involved and active.

1. Talking directly to the Audience

Most plays are performed as if there was nobody watching. The characters in them are unaware that they are being observed. This is not the case in a panto. Panto characters know full well that they are being watched and the audience is expected to become involved. In fact, the panto is written for that to happen. Here are four examples:

Number One – Introductions

When each major character first appears they introduce themselves (or are introduced by others). The Goodies want to meet and greet the audience. It's a matter of saying 'Hello' and its variants and encouraging the audience to respond. Plus, at the start of the panto, the audience is welcomed as well as given a bit of 'back story'. Here are two examples. The first is from 'Ali Baba and The Forty Thieves'.

Photo: The opening scene of 'Ali Baba', our first panto.

After the introductory song 'The Old Bazaar in Cairo'...

Ali Baba:
Welcome. Thrice welcome to Cairo. Ancient city of Egypt. Land of mystery and history, where Pharoahs rule and bellies dance. (holds nose) Sorry about The Sphinx!...Let me introduce myself. My name is Ali Baba. (bows) At your service. I'm a poor camel driver. And I drive a very poor camel...'

This scene setting 'meet and greet' moment can be extended and become a two-way process as happened in 'Dick Whittington' when Peggoty and Polyanthus Chinwag, the house staff of Alderman Fitzwarren, take to the stage. They are surprised by the audience being there.

Peggoty:
Oooh, hello. I'm Peggoty Chinwag.
Polyanthus:
And I'm her much more beautiful sister, Polyanthus.
Peggoty:
[not pleased] Oh, I like that!
Polyanthus:
[deliberately misunderstanding, refers to her outfit] Of course you do. [to Audience] As you can see, I am the one with class. My sister's so common. Not like what I am.
Peggoty:
Am I bovvered? Not no-how! Let me ajolopise for my older sister. She's going through a difficult time of life, if you get my drift.
Polyanthus:
You don't have to go telling everyone my hinnermost secrets! Just keep quiet for once in your life.
Peggoty:
It has been said that I like a bit of a natter.
Polyanthus:
That's not true. A bit of a natter is never enough for you! You're one for a full-blown no-holds-barred gossip, you are.

Peggoty:
　And you're not?... [to Audience] But before we go any further we need to know who you lot are.

Polyanthus:
　Yes, cos after all, we don't want to be strangers, do we? [aside to Peggoty] And there might be one or two edible battleships.

Peggoty:
　You what?

Polyanthus:
　You know. [suggestively] Edible battleships.

Peggoty:
　You mean eligible bachelors... you dumb cluck.

Polyanthus:
　What-ever.

Perggoty:
　[aside to Audience] I wouldn't say she was stupid, but when she went to a mind reader, he gave her her money back... Anyway, where were we? Oh, yes, getting to know you.

Polyanthus:
　[breaking into song] "Getting to know you. Getting to know all about you..."

Peggoty:
　[loudly to Audience, to cover the singing] At the count of three, all shout your names out. 1...2...3... [encourages Audience response] I didn't quite catch all of those. [to Polyanthus, who is coyly waving at a man in the Audience] Did you? [No response from Polyanthus] I said, did you catch anything?

Polyanthus:
　Not 'alf. I've caught a bit of a hunk in the third row and I'm just about to reel him in.

Peggoty:
　Not if his wife's got a say in the matter. [Polyanthus mouths a 'sorry' to man's wife.] [to Audience] We'd best have another go. At the count of 1...2...3...[At the end of this business, Peggoty addresses a different man in the Audience, whose name she seems to have heard.] Hello, Montmorency. You don't look much like a Montmorency to me, but then as I've never seen one

before, who knows what a Montmorency should look like.

Polyanthus:
[to another member of the Audience] Hello, Dame Sylvestra Slopbucket. It's a great pleasure, I'm sure. How's the singing going? Would you like me to give you a few tips?

Peggoty:
[to another member of the Audience] Lulu Lafontaine. Bonjewer. Common alley view. [She continues with a stream of comic 'French' noises.]

Polyanthus:
[to another member of the Audience, salutes] Major General Crispin Cholmondeley Walker. All present and correct, sir! I do like a forceful military man in uniform. [suggestively] With all his regalia!

Peggoty:
[to Polyanthus] Control yourself!

Polyanthus:
[pointing] I'd rather he did it for me.

Peggoty:
[to Audience] It's no good. This could take hours, and well, we don't want the pub to shut, do we? So...

Peggoty & Polyanthus:
Hello, EVERYONE!...

[And the scene finally moves on.]

Baddies need introductions too. This often takes the form of a warning from other characters as to their 'badness'. Here is an example from 'The Grand of Old Duchess of York'. It is the day of York Fair. A good time is being had when Albert, Archie and Arnold, three children, run on.

Albert:
Look out, everybody.

Archie:
Hide your money in your pockets.

Arnold:
And while you're at it, hide your pockets.

> Townsfolk:
> > [worried] You don't mean?
> Albert/Archie/Arnold:
> > Yes! It's her!
> Townsfolk:
> > Not Baroness Snatcher of Seizitt Hall!
> [On comes the lady with her gang of henchmen...]
> Baroness:
> > [to Townsfolk] Silence you pesky poltroons, you petty people, you pathetic peasants [to Audience who are booing] And as for you, you rustic rabble of numbskull nincompoops, stop sucking your thumbs and listen. [Audience boo some more.] Go on. [to henchmen] I was thinking about putting a tax on talking. I believe in freedom of expression, but it is a freedom you should pay for!...

By the way, here is an example of a sex-change character, as we reworked the typical Grand Old Duke into a Duchess (with a Baroness who was desperate to replace her). Years later we did another version where we had a real-life male Grand Old Duke trying his best to keep Baron Grabbit from getting his thieving hands on York!

Number Two – Re-introductions
Each time a major character returns he/she might well re-introduce themselves (especially if they haven't been seen for a while). In the case of Baddies they need to remind the audience of their badness. In the case of the Sheriff of Nottingham in 'Robin Hood' he sang:

> Boo me. Hiss me. Just to show you miss me. As long as you hate me, it's all right!

Number Three – Asking Questions
Often characters will ask the audience a question, and equally often this involves asking for help - help to find someone or to know if it's safe. It can be asking for the audience's opinion or approval; invariably The Dame will want to show off her outfit and expect praise in return!

Number Four – Seeking Sympathy

The character might be seeking sympathy – telling a bit of a sob story for the audience to 'Aaahh!' sympathetically in response. If the audience do not show sympathy, the character will repeat and explain the matter until they get the degree of sympathy they truly deserve.

You get the idea I hope.

2. Getting the Audience to participate as much as possible

> 'It would be nice if they laughed or reacted. Otherwise, why are we doing it?'
> [Lottie Hyde]

The cast needs to be reminded that though the script and storyline is well known to them, for the audience it will be totally new. Not only that, but the audience only has a short time to laugh/ groan/ cheer/ boo or whatever it is you would like them to do before the storyline moves on. So what can the cast do?

Number One - Give the Audience 'permission' or 'encouragement' to react.

From the outset the jokes need to be 'sold'. Here is an example from page 1 of 'Robin Hood'. Female Market Traders are discussing Life and Men:

> *Mrs Padlock:*
>   *Ladies, do you know the way to keep your youth?*
> *Traders:*
>   *No. What is the way to keep our youth?*
> *Mrs Padlock:*
>   *Lock him in your bedroom, and throw away the key.*
> *Mrs Padlock pauses.*

Version 1: If the audience groans, Mrs P adlibs with something like:

> *Sorry, but if you think that was a bad joke, there's much, much worse to come!*

Version 2: If the audience doesn't react, she repeats her joke and explains it in detail, finishing with,

Do you geddit? Good. Now, where were we?

In Version 1 the audience has its reaction accepted and included. In Version 2 the audience is given training in its role. The clear inference is that a reaction is expected from them.

The key was the 'pause', as it was in the romantic scene in 'Dick Whittington' we discussed earlier. Here it is serving a different purpose. How long should it be? This is very tricky to be precise about. The point is, if the character saying a line expects/hopes to get a laugh or a groan or some sort of audience reaction, he/she must give time for the reaction to come. If no time is given and the scene runs on, the audience will think that no reaction from them is called for.

Of course, members of the audience may well WANT to react, but aren't given the chance to really do so. There is nothing worse than when the audience starts to laugh, but the scene goes on without accepting it. The message from the stage appears to be, "Don't laugh. Just sit there and listen quietly." This is not the message we want to give out, is it?

Pauses are fundamentally important and need to be built in to the performance. They are not only used to give time for a reaction. They can be within speeches to give the audience time to process what's been said. Often the pause accompanied by a 'look' can be funnier than the line that preceded it.

Number Two – Asides
Asides allow a character to briefly turn away from the action on stage and address him/herself directly to the audience. In this way the audience is given the role of conspirator/ friend/ confessor and the relationship between the character and the audience is strengthened. We have seen asides being used earlier by Puss-in-Boots in 'Dick Whittington' when trying to manage Dick and Alice Fitzwarren. [See pages 51-53.] Here is an example from 'Robin Hood'.

Snow White has just met Robin Hood. She believes he is a woodcutter, who's about to cut down Sherwood Forest, and she is not amused. Robin is in part to blame because he has an axe. He is in disguise and toying with the idea of being a woodcutter as he has had enough of the 'do-gooding' business. That's why he has an axe, which he's swinging. Enough explanation. – Here's the scene...

> Robin:
> > Oww!
>
> Snow:
> > [angry] Are you a woodcutter?
>
> Robin:
> > I've got a splinter...It hurts.
>
> Snow:
> > Don't worry. [threatening] It'll hurt a whole lot more if you are a woodcutter! Are you?
>
> Robin:
> > It depends.
>
> Snow:
> > Depends on what?
>
> Robin:
> > **[aside to audience] Depends if she's about to hit me if I am.** [to Snow White] Depends who's asking.
>
> Snow:
> > I am Snow White.
>
> Robin:
> > [impressed] No way! Honestly? [Snow White nods.] Wow, if they could see me now, that little gang of mine. Here I am with the one and only ...Snow White. The Snow White! I mean, you're like mega famous. It's really great to know the Wicked Queen hasn't got her evil hands on you.
>
> Snow:
> > [unimpressed] Yes. Yes. Forget the Wicked Queen and all that mirror-mirror-on-the-wall stuff, who are you?
>
> Robin:
> > I'm Rob...[realises his mistake, adopts bad Scottish accent] Robert the Bruce. Och aye the noo! Lang may your lumb reek. Haggis and bagpipes and all that.

Snow:
> *[clearly disbelieving] So, Robert the Bruce, what are you doing in Sherwood Forest, and are you a woodcutter?* **[aside to audience] I really hope he isn't one, because he's quite ... you know, isn't he?** *[turns serious again] And have you seen Robin Hood?...*

Number Three – Adlibs

We've heard about them already. Some cast like them. Others, less so. Sometimes the writer sets out to encourage them. What are they? They are unscripted lines of dialogue (not written by the writer) added by the actor in the guise of the character he/she is playing, or they can be out of character comments. Here are examples of both.

In 'Robin Hood' The Big Bad Wolf is trying to get The Three Little Pigs back to his place for the obvious reasons – He's a hungry wolf and they are three prize porkers. He has heard Porcina, Winona and Bettina singing, and is now pretending to look for the 'mystery' singers in order to make them famous. Enough said.

Porcina:
> *Who are you looking for?*

Wolf:
> *What do you mean who am I looking for? Don't just stand there like so much ham on the hock, start searching.*

Winona:
> *[following, searching] Who are we looking for?*

Wolf:
> *Angels, that's who! Are you deaf or something? You must have heard them?*

Bettina:
> *Heard who?*

Wolf:
> *The next Big Thing, that's who! Simon will kill me if I tell him I've let such talent slip through my claws... [correcting self] my fingers.*

Winona:
> *Simon?*

Wolf:
> *Simon. Simon Bowel. The Great Mover! [explains joke to Audience]...*

And this is where the script as written stopped, encouraging the person playing the Wolf to wing it and be creative. He stepped out of Wolf character and went on something like this:

Wolf:
> *I'm sorry about that cheap joke. I mean, 'Bowel'. 'The Great Mover'. It is quite degrading for an actor of my standing, after a career treading the boards, to have to work with this kind of material. I told the writer that the Audience wouldn't like it, but would he listen? Of course not. So there we are. Bowel. Bodily function. The Great Mover. Need I say more? Shakespeare it is not! ... Now where was I?*

And so he returned to the script as written and the scene continued.

Adlibs can also be used to embellish the written lines or at moments when the real lines don't come to mind.

Adlibs are also a topic of sometimes heated discussion and opposing views.

> 'One time we had Hugh Fearnley-Whittingstall in the audience and John as The Wolf changed the script in the evening. In the matinee he had this cookbook and suddenly in the evening it was Hugh F-W's cookbook. And I was waiting for my cue and it didn't come because the script had been totally changed to suit one member of the audience! Albeit a famous person. Fun, but it was confusing.'
> [Alan Clark]

📷 Photo: The Wolf and his lair.

And in spite of what fellow actors or the Director might think, the Audience can think differently when it comes to adlibbing.

'As an audience it's lovely when they go off track. You can tell they're doing it. Yet they do it really well and it adds to it.'
[Becky Fooks]

Act Five – Scene Two: One Day To Go! – The Dress Rehearsal

This is in essence a dry run with everything in place except the audience.

Here are our rules for a successful Dress Rehearsal.

- It should be run as if it were a performance.

- Everybody must be present (including all the production and backstage staff).

- Everybody must be fully ready to start at the starting time. This may mean turning up quite early in the case of people with complex costumes to get into or make-up to put on.

- Ensure that photographs are taken. We always do this before starting. This encourages everyone to be fully ready.

- Everybody is responsible for knowing where their props are and checking them. [For Props go to Act Seven: Scene Three, pages 168-169.]

- The Dress Rehearsal will not stop for any reason other than a major one as decided by the Director.

- If people forget their lines, they or other members of cast need to deal with it. [We have only once had a prompter in 10 pantos, and we have found that the cast copes very well without one.]

- All entrances and exits must be from wherever they will be during the actual performance.

- There must be quiet off-stage.

- Costumes, set and props must all be respected by the cast. Costumes need to be neatly re-hung when taken off. Sets and props are not to be treated roughly. They all have to be used again and still look good.

- Have an interval. Provide refreshments. Get cast to order whatever drinks they would like during the Interval on show day(s).

- Concentration is the keyword. Each cast member needs to take responsibility for what they need to do.

- Go through the bows at the end. Ensure that the sequence is well understood. Provide a list in the wings as a reminder.

Setting up Changing Rooms - Getting into Costume

'It was the first time you see people's costumes. We'd all go and look at each other and have hysterics! The ladies who've made costumes over the years have done a fantastic job. We never used to fork out a lot of money. Years ago when we all used to do dressmaking we'd have remnants. That gold Fairy Godmother dress was one I'd found somewhere in a charity shop. The other time I made a lurex-y silver one. I don't remember what I said, but I remember what I wore!'
[Beryl Banks]

Some cast come in costume fully made-up. Some come in make-up and partly changed. Others need to change completely and have make-up applied. As per previous instructions they head off to allocated changing areas/dressing rooms. These have been determined by the Production Assistants after looking at the facilities available at the venue and at the needs of the cast. Each designated changing room/space has a list of who should be there. For example: all children under 11 are together in Changing Room 1. All teenage boys and adult men are together in Changing Room 2. All teenage girls and adult women are together in Changing Room 3. Or something like that. Whatever seems most appropriate.

And it is only now that the cast get the overall impact of what the panto is going to look like. Many of them have already seen their own costumes, or bits and pieces of them, but now it all comes together.

What about the Dame if 'she' is being played by a man? Where does he/she change? The Dame is going to need space. Her outfits are always going to be large and quite probably difficult to get into. To do so, she is going to need help. The Dame can come to the venue in full make-up, but cannot arrive in costume. That is not on. So, like I say, she needs space. Maybe your venue has space for the Dame to have to herself. If not, and if it is OK with the women in your cast, the Dame could change in the female changing room.

> 'John Davies became an honorary female as he was playing the panto Dame. This meant much hilarity in the women's room as we all fussed over him and helped him on with his costume and make-up. He had to borrow false eyelash glue from Snow White because his had dried up!'
> [Leigh Carroll-Smith]

And when any of our panto Dames appears before the rest of the cast in full rig the effect is usually jaw-dropping.

> 'At the time of Andrew asking me to be The Dame I was aware of a friend of mine in Crewkerne, who features as The Dame just about every year. So I had a quick chat to him. And it was at that point he offered me the loan of a very large chest! I believe it was quoted as a 55inch pair of

gazonkas, or something like that. It was very good of him to let me borrow them because that solved one problem!'
[John Davies, who was Mother Hood in 'Robin Hood'.]

📷 Photo: Mother Hood and the Market Traders.

Moving to the children's Changing Room. Here the costumes have been set out character by character and a Production Assistant (in our case a village childminder) has the responsibility for ensuring they get changed correctly. In some cases the youngest children will probably need help.

Make-Up

'Matthew's mum did the make-up and we all started laughing when we saw each other backstage. We had red cheeks and freckles.'
[Emily Chubb as Hatter, a dwarf]

There are several schools of thought regarding stage make-up and we tend to do a bit of everything. In general terms this is what we think:

1. The Dame is in full OTT make-up, loud, luscious, colourful, with wig and the longest eyelashes wearable! He/she needs someone who knows what they are doing to work with him/her as helper/dresser. [See Mother Hubbard in close-up on Front Cover photograph.]

2. Women playing more regular characters wear a (slightly) exaggerated version of normal full female make-up, bold enough to be able to be seen under strong stage lights. They happily do their own or help each other.

3. As for the men in the cast, most are happiest without any basic make-up. But they do like the idea of having scars, blacked-out teeth, warts, false noses and the like. If the Baddies are men, they certainly need something from that list. Women playing certain types of Baddies like to put on similar disguises where appropriate.

4. And now the children. We always ensure that they remain children. We never give any of the girls make-up that could be construed as turning them into mini-adults, even if they might like the idea. Ruddy cheeks and freckles can be used for almost any character that the young children are playing! If you have someone who does face painting, that is most helpful.

5. Characters playing animals – sheep, cats, wolves and the like – are probably being costumed in ways that suggest they are animals. In the case of sheep, they might wear white knitted balaclavas with ears.

The cats have mittens and tails. And the Wolf is dressed like a country gent with furry gloves and a trilby hat with ears attached. His tail is sewn to his tweed trousers. The audience knows what they are and so their make-up suggests their animal nature in the same way. White faces with black noses for sheep. Brown noses with painted on whiskers for cats. Black nose surrounded by black spots for the Wolf. This 'token' make-up works very well.

Once changed and made up, cast come together for photos and a chat from the Director, who sets out the goals for the evening. And it is nearly time to start.

A star is born!

Aside Seventeen – Comment

Late on in the rehearsal period – say a week or so before the first performance (though it might be as late on as the day itself) – cast members take full ownership of their performances. They have taken on board what the Director has been banging on about for weeks. And now they have shaped it into something far more personal to themselves. This is proof positive that they are now confident in what they are doing and having fun. The Dress Rehearsal sets out to demonstrate this. By the following day, the day of the performance, the panto is not the Director's, it is theirs!

Notes

📷 Photo: Director giving notes.

Cast want and need feedback, but how depends on the Director and the style he/she has. Bringing the cast together at the end of the rehearsals and giving them your thoughts, etc, and asking for any thoughts from those present, is one way. Some people prefer to give out notes in written form (though nothing stops you from emailing or texting). I give verbal notes most of the time, but probably hand out brief written notes before the Big Rehearsals (Technical and Dress) in order to remind people of certain key things and also to gee them up to make just a bit more effort.

Cast members will also assess their own performances and can be quite hard on themselves.

> 'The worst bit was the Dress Rehearsal on the Friday night when I couldn't remember any of my lines. And I thought: "Oh, dear. Should I have entered into this?" I was a bit cheesed off with myself. Cos you feel you're letting other people down when you don't get your lines out.'
> [John Davies]

An old stage adage says: 'A Bad Dress Rehearsal means a Great Performance!' As a Director that is something to cling on to if things have not gone well. Conversely, if the Dress Rehearsal has been a triumph, it may lead to false confidence.

Let's be absolutely clear about the purpose of the Dress Rehearsal; it is to show the cast that they can do it, that they are ready. Yes, there might have been one or two glitches, but as long as everyone was giving it their all, the Director has nothing more to ask of them. Other, than to have a grand time when the curtain goes up on Show Day.

ACT SIX

Including: Business. Publicity, promotion, and getting punters through the door. Ticket Selling: 'How to get bums on seats'.

Business: Getting an Audience

So we are very close to our performance(s). But there is no point putting on a panto without an audience. But who is your audience? And how can you go about getting people through the doors to see your pantos?

Act Six – Scene One: Publicity, promotion, and getting punters through the doors

How big is your potential audience? This determines so much of what you will do. Before you start promoting your panto, before you spend time and money printing tickets, and certainly before you start selling them, you need to be absolutely sure of the seating capacity of the venue. This will be specified in the venue's performing licence or insurance certification. A failure to comply would mean you are contravening Fire Regulations – and that is something you definitely don't want to do.

So, let's say you learn that the venue has a seating capacity of 200. Does it actually have 200 seats? If not, are you willing to borrow/hire/transport the shortfall? Then again, with the way that you are staging your panto, will there be room to put out 200 seats (if you have them)? Don't go packing the venue with seats and then find that people cannot move about easily and safely. An audience that cannot move is not a happy one! Think about the Interval when you are hoping to provide refreshments (and incidentally make money), you want there to be space for everyone to be served relatively efficiently. Early in the rehearsal period we set out the auditorium with seats to see just how many tickets we are going to be able to sell. If you do likewise, think seriously about legroom. We have all travelled on budget airlines and moaned about cramped conditions. You don't want your audience packed in like sardines, do you? [Oh, no you don't!]

We have learned over the years that of the 280 tickets we sell on average, well over 200 of them are sold to adults, a lot of whom come without children. Of the children there are usually about 30 or so aged under 5. So they are our audience. They are our villagers, naturally, but they are from neighbouring villages, too. Then there are the friends and relatives of our cast, some of whom come a long way to be with us. It can be surprising just how far grandparents are ready to travel in order to see their grandchildren on stage, or how far daughters will drive if there is the chance of seeing their father playing The Dame!

Does your venue have provision for people with mobility issues? Does it have a disabled access, a ramp, a disabled toilet? If it does, and you have audience members who are wheelchair users, what kind of space will they require?

These are the people of our audience and they need tickets. But at what ticket price? This is something for each community to decide for itself. We have three categories of ticket. They are adults, children from 5 to 16, and children under 5 years old. The under-5s don't pay. They have free tickets. Why have we always done this?

- We want young children to get the panto bug as early as possible.

- The very young often spend much of the show on a knee and not on a seat.

📷 Photo: On the knee and enthralled.

- Sometimes the very young spend time outside the venue 'recovering' from the atmosphere. Having a Wolf growl at you can be more than you can take when you're two years old.

You can never predict how the youngest in your audience are going to react.

> 'I remember Jack getting a laugh as a little-un in the audience. Then he didn't really like pantos. He didn't wanna be there. He was struggling and sitting underneath a chair. Dr John (as the Baddie) at the end of the panto was going for the great "Ah-hah! We're all finished now and I'm done for" bit. And Jack managed to get in: "Oh, good. Can we go home now?" Poor old John lost his last laugh, because Jack had it!'... So we knew at some time he had to be on the stage.'
> [Mark House]

All members of your audience need a ticket. In this way you will know how many people you are performing to, you can be sure of numbers in case of any emergency, and the refreshment team will know how many they need to cater for. You certainly do not want them running out of tea, squash, wine, biscuits and the like! If that happens, you have both the audience and the refreshment team on your back.

Producing tickets

The simplest method can be totally homemade. Something printable using a laptop, for example, is quite sufficient and low cost. You can print off as many as you need as you go. These tickets can be of one type, but with boxes to tick stating the date/time of performance (if you are performing more than once), and for stating the category of ticket holder, eg: adult, child, under-5.

Alternatively your Box Office Manager might want to be more creative and have different ticket types for each performance and each category. This means three types of ticket per performance. It looks more professional, but is more expensive and more time consuming. It also means that in order not to waste ink and card, printing can only happen in response to demand.

You might like to think about numbered tickets, too.

Having tickets printed professionally incurs a significant cost and probably is unnecessary unless you are selling in large numbers.

Act Six – Scene Two: Ticket Selling: 'How to get bums on seats'

We know who our audience is going to be. Barring a small number, they are people within a few miles of the village, or people with direct links to our community. This is the case for many community ventures. How do they know about the panto and how do we sell to them?

Cast members and panto staff are the most important agents for promotion and ticket selling. As the weeks of rehearsal pass cast spread the word, often 'over the garden fence', or its modern equivalent. Who knows someone might even tweet! Word of Mouth is proved to be the most effective way of getting information out there. Then, if you have a cast of about 40 (as we usually do) all you need is for each one to sell 2 to 3 tickets and you've sold over 100 already. Of course, not everyone can sell. After all some of your cast are young children. But having our cast sell a minimum of 100 tickets is always our goal. How do we sell the rest?

We use very few other methods. We put up A4

size posters in surrounding villages and in certain places in local towns. These require designing, printing and displaying, but we do not use very many. We feel they act as memory joggers. We send out copy to local free press or to local magazines, which have a free community ads section. But we do nothing more adventurous. That is not to say that you shouldn't. It depends on what you feel will work for you. If you have a volunteer who is enthusiastic and willing to take on board the role of promoting your panto in other ways, all power to you. But never forget the number of tickets you have to sell and balance that with the effort being made to sell them.

Poster designs by Hazel Yates-Jones: Ali Baba in 1993; Mother Hubbard in 1998

So, back to the job of selling those tickets the cast aren't busy selling. This is where the Box Office comes in. If you are going to publicise your panto (via a newsletter, on posters, free newspapers, village website, online blog, on local radio, etc), you need a contact number if nothing else for people to order tickets. For the actual act of selling tickets you need a Box Office Manager — a methodical person with a good business head — who is willing to deal with bookings. This might sound wonderfully straightforward. It is if there is a clear system in place, which everyone follows. But a community panto is not run like a professional enterprise. Nor are the majority of your audience typical theatre-goers.

The Box Office Manager wants the following:

- A booking form, which is easy to fill in and widely available.

- Once filled in the form should be returned to the address on the form with a cheque made payable to the Panto Society or whichever organisation is handling the income. This, of course, has to be an organisation with a bank account.

- People to arrange to pick up their booked tickets.

But if people ring up or email to book tickets, the system begins to get a bit more complex. For one thing there is no accompanying money up front. So now when people come to pick up their tickets there is the matter of payment and this could take the form of cash or cheque.

And then there is the matter of people placing phone or email bookings, but failing to collect. Now the number of booked tickets is growing, but the money doesn't match. The Box Office Manager begins to twitch.

And then some people want to collect their tickets on the day of the performance at the venue 'on the door'. They have any one of a hundred different reasons for being unable to get to the Ticket Office. Can we trust them to come on the day? If not, we have lost income, because we could possibly have sold those tickets to other people.

And so it goes on. Tickets are sold, and your audience grows larger. We always begin to take bookings early in the rehearsal period. Why? For everyone engaged in making the panto happen it focuses the mind to know that 50 tickets have already gone, or 100, or more. For those cast members who might be adopting a relaxed attitude to the task of learning their lines it delivers a coldwater shock of reality. Yes, the panto is really going to happen, and there will be real people in large numbers out front waiting to be entertained... Pause for the light of realisation to dawn (or the penny to drop).

MEANWHILE, back behind the scenes...

ACT SEVEN

Including: Getting Technical. Sound. Lights. Props. Production Assistants.

Getting Technical

While the rehearsal period has moved on and we are moving ever closer to the date(s) of performance what has been happening on the technical side of things?

📷 Photo: Our technicians in the lighting gallery.

Act Seven – Scene One: Sound

Here we move into the wonderful world of creative sound effects (SFX). Of course, there are some realistic sound effects that can be made live. In fact, they are best done live. For example, if a character is going to press a button for a realistic-sounding doorbell, such a doorbell could be built in to the set. Or if a character is going to ring a hand bell, have him do it for real. In both cases using real things to make the sounds live on stage means that accurate cueing is never going to be a problem. But if you want a spooky gothic doorbell to sound when the character presses the button, that is when you need to use a pre-recorded effect.

Quite early in the rehearsal period the Director sits with the technical whizz and talks through his/her wish list of sounds, the more bizarre the better as far as I'm concerned. For several years Norman Marsden, a retired electrical/electronic engineer, has been faced with a raft of odd panto requests. He appreciates the challenge they give him.

This is his account of making, as he says,...

'Strange Noises in the Village Hall'

'Although I had some experience in audio recording and microphone placement, sound effects was something I had never attempted before 2007.

So where to start? I had some old 45rpm records with a range of sound effects, which were of limited use. But a search of the web did produce a vast range of sounds most of which cost money. So I concentrated on the free sounds and short samples.

Getting the right sound to match the script proved more difficult than I imagined and Andrew and I auditioned lots of 'noises' and rejected many of them. I tried recording real sounds without much success until I installed a sound editing application on my PC; this enabled me to modify sounds by changing the speed and pitch, adding echo and then combining a number of the sound recordings together to produce a finished result which would be acceptable. But many times the result was feeble and useless and had to be rejected.

'The Magic Cupboard' in 2009 was the second pantomime for which I managed the sound and produced some sound effects including a clock striking, doors creaking, fireworks and cheering, a bubbling cauldron and a cow bellowing! Additionally there was some musical extracts to play during various scenes. Some of these sounds were to be used more than once during the performance.

Having spent some time in editing the sounds, the next move was to rehearse with the cast. This opened my eyes (ears?) to the next stumbling block – playing the right sounds on cue and how long to play the sounds for. The main problem is that no two performances are the same; the cast may not stick to their lines. Or they may be late or early appearing on stage. And interaction with audience may mean adlibbing and resuming the script at a random place. This presents a real challenge and means making a snap judgement when to start and stop a sound, or even to miss it out altogether. In any case I had to carefully tailor the start time and duration of each sound to try to cope with these variations.

The equipment I decided to use was a laptop PC installed with playing software which allowed each sound file to be played rapidly i.e. with the minimum use of keyboard and mouse. This worked well with 'The Magic Cupboard' allowing for the odd mis-timings. Fortunately the audience does not have a copy of the script, so the 'goofs' may go unnoticed.

Although the sound effects worked well, they were played through the Hall public address loudspeakers located at the sides of the Hall. This helped with voices, but did not give the best sense of location of sound effects. The sounds should come from the stage where the action is set, and the solution was to locate a loudspeaker at the stage area for sound effects only.'

As Norman says, these days there are any number of websites where you can download free effects or others at a small cost. It can be a bit odd sitting and listening to noises and then talk about their relative merits: "Which loud crash sounded funniest?" "Does that really sound like comic vomit?" Our pantos always call for 'comic falls', 'spooky atmosphere', 'baddie entrances', 'crashes and collisions', 'romantic theme', and never forget 'chases, short or long'. There are others, but variants of these basic ones are always needed. By the way, when it comes to a theme to accompany chases it is hard to beat 'Yakety-sax', used by the late Benny Hill for all his speeded up chases. If it was good enough for him, it is good enough for us nine times out of ten.

Of course you might be able to call upon the talents of a silent movie-type pianist and not need SFX for your scene-setting. However, even the most skilled pianist is hard put to come up with a truly 'comic crash'.

It is fair to say that both the cast and the audience love the fun and foolishness that good SFX can add. They help to create the whacky panto world your characters inhabit.

Norman refers to the real challenge for your SFX technician - getting the timing right. He/she needs a full script marked with the sound plot, telling him/her exactly when to play what during the panto and for how long. Correct cueing needs to be sorted out during the Technical Rehearsal. But, as Norman points out, nothing is truly fixed as performers can be very creative when it comes to giving a performance!

If you are using microphones, these need to be controllable. During Front of Curtain scenes and the Interval when sets and/or scenery are being changed behind the curtains, the last thing you want is to have this amplified over the public address system. So the turning on and off of these mikes needs to be cued on the sound plot. [See Appendix III for an extract from the combined Sound and Lighting Plot for 'Robin Hood'.]

Act Seven – Scene Two: Lights

If only two things make a panto special, one of them is costume, the other is the change from light to darkness and back again to light. When the houselights go down (= are switched off) the audience's attention is grabbed and their expectations rise. So, every panto needs lights and the more the better. How? If the venue already has some stage lights rigged, that is great. If not, you should seriously think about borrowing or hiring some. Depending on the size of your stage, even as few as four stage lights make all the difference. Installing them is a job for someone who knows what they are doing.

We have always had Ken Banks, an electrician, doing our lights. Over to him:

> 'We started off using a lighting gallery to the right hand side of the stage as you look at it, which was very cramped, with ordinary switches controlling Pattern 23 lamps – lights which were in fact about 60 to 70 years old...'

This gallery was in fact nothing more than a shelf or ledge above the doorway leading downstairs, which offered a sideways squinting view of the stage. Ken perched there a bit like a hen in a henhouse. Back to him:

> 'After 2 or 3 years probably – I can't exactly remember when – we built a lighting gallery at the far end of the Hall, over the entrance doors, so you could sit there and look directly at the stage and operate the lighting.
>
> Then, of course, we had to alter all the wiring for the stage lighting, rewiring it to the other end of the Hall. We then hired in various lights when we needed `em, which was a bit of a pain in the neck – having to collect `em and take `em back when we finished with `em. So we thought it'd be more sense to have our own lights. So the profits from all the pantomimes up to then were put to one side within the Village Hall Fund for when we had enough to be able to buy ourselves the proper lighting scheme. Then we received a grant of a thousand pounds from Artsreach (= the rural arts scheme for Dorset) and then we got various moneys from other funds and people raised money as well. We eventually went out and bought 8 new 650watt lights with barn doors and provision to put coloured filters in them, and a 12-way Lighting Dimmer Rack with a Dimmer Console Control. This is computerised (not that I've learned how to use that yet!) We've got 12 circuits on there that we can double up. And that controller could actually – because it's on a long lead – be taken out of the Lighting Gallery and used down on the Hall floor. So someone who was disabled, and who was gonna control the lighting, and couldn't get up into the Lighting Gallery (which involves climbing a ladder) could control the lights from down below from their wheelchair. A bit of forethought! Hopefully I shan't have to use it!

Photo: View from Lighting Gallery.

Some of the lights you can turn them from big floods into spots. We use those mainly on the front row (= nearest the stage) to light the front of the stage. Then we use all the old lights – that we haven't thrown away because they still work – until we can afford something better – we use those above the stage and some in the centre of the Hall for doing directional runabout scenes, and creating atmosphere in the body of the Hall. The dead blackout option on the lighting is good because it kills the lighting immediately and then can restore it straight away without having the lights dimming down or up. `Cos usually when you fade lights in and out you're taking a lighting effect away gradually, so that people don't notice it. For example, changing day into night like the sun going down and then in the morning you pull the lights back up again.'

What do you need for a show to go smoothly, Ken?

'We need to know what the cast are doing, meaning we have to watch the show through beforehand so that we can learn and anticipate what they are going to do; so that we're ready to bring up lights or take lights out as required for whatever scene – to put things into darkness or lighten up certain parts. We then set the stage and you draw up a lighting plot so that I know which lights to switch on and off at which times – to make the thing come to life.'

From my point of view, when it comes to The Show, what makes a place a 'theatre' is darkness. It goes black. And immediately you know a) we're in a place where there's going to be a show, and b) there's that instant expectation. And what do you think, Ken?

'The stage is like the end of the tunnel. Put light at the end of the tunnel. People are focussed instead of just sitting there. So it's helping the people on the stage get their part across. They've got the audience watching them because the audience can't see anything else and are not distracted. I always feel it's better when there's plenty of effects. They keep the audience wondering what's happening next. It can also be used to disguise things. If the light is there and the audience is watching, something else can be happening in the darkness; backstage people could be doing a set change.'

Picking up on things mentioned by Ken:

When lighting a panto, you will need a session where the Director and Lighting Technician rig the lights so that all of the stage is lit as evenly as possible, downstage (front), upstage (back) and the corners. Don't waste light by lighting areas that are not being used; try to reduce light spill as much as you can. You can test evenness of illumination by walking across the stage crabwise (facing out to the audience). This reveals any areas of shadow or faded brightness on the person as they go across.

The Director needs to go through the Lighting Plot with the Lighting Technician before the Technical Rehearsal (= the Tech). In order to draw up this plot you need to know the numbering system relating to the dimmer rack. Each light or maybe each pair of lights lights a specific part of the stage. And each light (or pair) has a different control, each with its own number. The plot needs to be written in a clear, simple, easy to follow fashion.

The Tech might be the first time the Lighting Technician will have had the chance to work the lights, though if he/she has been able to attend a rehearsal before the Tech, that is most helpful. Getting lighting cues right is a must, just as it is with sound cues. Remember that these cues might not be lines of dialogue, but the entrance of a character, an exit, a bit of physical business, or after a pause. For example when the hero grabs the hands of his true love everyone expects a lighting change and romantic music to well up. If this doesn't happen, we all feel a bit cheated – cast and audience alike.

Your venue is probably not a theatre, but you want to create as near a theatrical atmosphere as you can. Lights are key to this. However, you need to be aware that as your venue probably has windows (unlike a theatre) you could well have a problem with daylight seeping in. If you are performing in the afternoon or on an evening in spring, you will definitely have this to think about. If your venue has typical windows (recessed, with window ledges), the simplest solution is to make screens from sheet cardboard, which can be placed at each window. We used this solution for a number of years until the venue installed roller blinds.

And in a performance there is a major advantage to having good stage lighting from a cast point of view. With lights in their eyes, 'You forgot there was loads of people in front of you.' [Jo House]

[See Appendix III for an extract from the combined Sound and Lighting Plot for 'Robin Hood'.]

Act Seven – Scene Three: Props

'I remember making that lovely giant birthday cake that Mike had to fall into, face first.'
[Mary Trott]

Props volunteers

Props are the portable bits and pieces used by characters. Some are personal to one character. Others are of more general use. In the case of many personal props we encourage (expect) the person playing the part (or another cast member) to provide them, especially if they aren't integral to the scene as written, but are instead, in a way, supplementary to the costume. Examples would be spectacles for the Old Duke, a feather duster for Ada the Maid, a wooden spoon for Mavis the Cook, or a fan for Lady Crabapple. Other more panto-specific personal props need to be found, made or bought. Examples of these are axes for the Lumberjacks, a sceptre for King Pippin, a scroll for the Witch, and wands for the Fairies.

Then there are other props, which are used by more than a single character, and, like the Witch's scroll, are absolutely fundamental to the plot. Examples are all the treasure found by Ali Baba, the range of food served up by Mother Hood, and the cargo loaded by the crew of 'The Saucy Sal'. Some can be found. Others need to be made. The making, borrowing and buying are the responsibility of your Props Manager (who in our case is also in charge of Costumes). She/he would benefit from a team of helpers maybe brought together for a Props Making Workshop, when a lot can be done in a relatively short time. [Refer to Jenny Beck's advice in Act Three: Scene Two, page 88.]

Keeping tabs on props during rehearsals (and in time, during performances) is another job for the Production Assistants or Props Manager. Cast need to be reminded often that if the prop is broken or goes missing they are going to look silly without it on stage. Allocating labelled trays to cast members, in which they should find and to which they should return their props after use, is a good idea. But they will need training!

It is very unlikely that the real props will be available from the start of the rehearsal period. Until they are ready, dummy props should be used. Simple sticks can be wands, axes, cutlasses, truncheons, or even a trumpet. Crockery, pots and pans from the venue's kitchen can stand in for royal goblets, a witch's cauldron or all of the bits and pieces required at The Three Little Pigs' picnic. It doesn't matter that the dummy prop bears little if any resemblance to the real prop, it gets the cast used to using something - to picking it up, holding it, passing it, putting it down, remembering where it is and where it should end up. The point is, the sooner cast stop miming that they are using something, and use something (anything), the better.

Act Seven – Scene Four: Production Assistants

Without one or more than one right-hand women (or men) the Director would lose the plot entirely! Like a lifejacket for a sailor, do not start out without one. The ideal Production Assistant is methodical, adept at forward planning, able to be diplomatic, hard working, organised, great at setting up workable systems and at explaining them. In short, they are the kind of PA that most of us would like helping us manage our normal day-to-day lives. In panto-land the Production Assistants keep the whole show on track. While the Director is having another 'great idea', they are making notes and coming up with a way that will make the 'great idea' a reality. They are the glue that binds all the bits and pieces together.

Here are some key guidelines on their role:

> 'Be sensitive to the Director's state of mind – know when to back off. Take on tasks, which do not require artistic dimensions. Be aware that what the Director thinks is a simple task – "anyone could do it" – is not always so. Make tea. Keep abreast of changes to script, stage directions, rehearsal schedule, everything.'
> [Rosemary Shepherd]

That's exactly it! Production Assistants need to be involved in everything. And keeping abreast of all changes throughout the rehearsal period is most important. But 'everything' may be a bit too vague. Here is a list bringing together much of what appears at other times in this book:

- attend rehearsals.

- help prepare space before rehearsals.

- keep a 'master script' up-to-date.

- provide 'dummy' props for use in rehearsal.
- set up a system for managing real props.
- shepherd the youngest children throughout the panto period.
- rehearse lines with cast members.
- run scenes that have already been set by the Director.
- act as a prompter in rehearsals.
- offer help wherever and whenever it is needed.
- set up changing rooms.
- check names for programme.
- set up a cast sign-in register on Show Day.
- check facilities of the venue before the Show – doors, toilets, seating, signage, heating, etc.
- liaise with Director, sharing Show Day tasks and responsibilities as appropriate.
- liaise with Front of House Staff, Technicians and Refreshment Staff on Show Day.
- check set and stage lay-out with Director on Show Day.
- help with 'The Day After' – dismantling, removing, returning, discarding, clearing, etc after the panto is finished.

and

- make tea.

'At one particular rehearsal we all turned up looking like Nanook of the North as we were in the middle of a snowstorm. Rosemary came to the rescue with cups of tea and coffee.'
[Leigh Carroll-Smith]

Who knows, one day a Production Assistant could take over the directorial baton from the Director. It's a thought. You might find that this offers a solution when the Director finally wants to put himself out to pasture. Training up someone to take over would be great if it is at all possible.

ACT EIGHT

Including: Extras. The Programme. Front of House. Refreshments. Bar. Making Keepsakes.

Act Eight: Extras

> 'The panto show itself is a central part of a bigger thing. There are the people who make the costumes, the make-up assistants, people who lend equipment, people who stand on the door, people who operate the bar, the kitchen, clean – loads of people involved. Not necessarily star performers. But they are there. And you can't really achieve what we achieved without those people.'
> [Danny Kirk]

The day has come. You have an audience. They have needs, even if they don't know it yet. And, of course, you have a cast who have needs too.

Act Eight – Scene One: The Programme

The audience expects a programme and the cast like to see their names in print. But that is not all. The Programme is where the production announces the names of everybody who has helped make it a success. And the names need to be right. Nobody can be miss-spelt or omitted. Regarding getting names right, I still remember an occasion when I gave some children the wrong surname as I failed to be aware of the family set-up. In this world of stepfamilies and others, never assume. If you don't really know, check. And even if you're sure, check.

The cast list of characters' names set against who is playing them comes first. You might need to give a few words of description against certain characters, eg:

Mother Aubergine Hubbard (boarding house keeper)
Tom Piper, her eldest son
Peter Piper, her younger son
Georgie Porgie, her beau

After the full cast list, the programme needs to list all the names of people from within the community who have worked on the production or helped in any other way. From the beginning of the panto-making process, the panto team-leaders, for example the Costume Chief and the Set Designer need to be keeping a list of everyone who is helping. Your team could be fulfilling any of the following roles.

Prompter
Music
Choreography
Stage Design & Construction
Scenery & Artwork
Props
Costume Design & Making
Make-up
Lights
Sound
Box Office
Publicity
Front of House
Refreshments & Bar
Production Assistants
Script
Direction

The list is as long as it needs to be for everyone in your panto to receive their mention. You will find that some names appear more than once. So be it. And that is not all, because you need a section dedicated to 'thanks', naming which people or whatever agencies have helped provide anything.

The more names in the programme, the stronger the message is that the panto is a community-made production.

When it comes to format, you can go for the simple one sheet A4, single or double-sided, black on white. It clearly is the simplest and therefore the least expensive to produce. Even printing the programme yourselves, there is a cost involved. If you are paying for the printing to be done professionally, the cost is more, of course, but the product will possibly look better.

So you have your programme. Do you charge for them or are they free to your audience? We have always gone for a simple format and then charged 20p per programme, which covers the cost of printing and gives a small profit and so adds to the panto income. How many you print is another thing to think about. You don't want to run out and you don't want to have lots left over. For an audience of 280 we find 90 is enough.

Act Eight – Scene Two: Front of House

In the run up to the performance you need to recruit volunteers to be your Front of House staff. The number required depends on the size of venue and therefore the size of your audience. After audience have been dealt with by Box Office they become the responsibility of the Front of House staff. What are their roles?

- to meet and greet.
- to respond to any specific needs.
- to guide audience to available seats.
- to keep a check on empty seats.
- to negotiate between audience members in order to make the best use of the seating.
- to sell programmes, so they will need a cash float.

- to clear away anything that might endanger, eg: abandoned crockery, handbags and the like cluttering aisles.

- to liase with the Director/Production Assistants, especially in the last few minutes before the scheduled start times, at the beginning of the panto and after the interval.

- to switch off/on house lights as and when needed, unless this can be done by the Lighting Technician.

In short their role is to manage the 'theatrical space' and the audience once it is in the auditorium.

To do this job you need volunteers who are aware, who are skilled at dealing with people, who are friendly and diplomatic, but able to be firm. They need to be able to deal with all the nerves, which are all around them, not least in the audience where proud relatives are crowded in and wanting their family members to do well in the panto that is soon to start.

Aside Nineteen – Car Parking

Does your venue have its own car park? Does it have signs? Is there space enough for both cast and audience to park their cars? If the answer is 'yes' to these questions, then you can relax. If not, you have to act to avoid gridlock. Maybe you could think about the following.

- Setting up signage.

- Roping off areas where parking is not to be allowed.

- Requesting cast not to park their cars at the venue on show day.

- Setting up a drop-off point.

- Locating/providing alternative off-road parking.

- Speaking to The Highways Authority and/or the police.

- Having volunteers to man whatever car parking is available.

Act Eight – Scene Three: Refreshments

We have space enough in our venue to run soft refreshments and the bar separately. We have found this works to speed serving. We run the bar only in the evening, which is the second of our two performances, and when we have a predominantly adult audience.

Ahead of time the people in charge of soft refreshments need to have a cash float for the purchase of tea, milk, etc. On the day they need a system in place to cater to the audience (and cast) during the interval. Drimpton has a name locally for delivering excellent food – it is very rare for any village event not to have great homemade food at its heart. However, on the occasion of pantos, it is necessary to 'keep it simple'. Tea. Coffee. Squash. Biscuits. Interval time is limited to about 20mins which is too short for making tasty treat choices. It also generates more crockery to collect and clear from the area before the panto can resume.

So our advice is for hot and cold drinks with the option of biscuits. Have a set price, for example 50p. This speeds up the payment process. In our matinees, when we have a large number of children present, we offer squash for free.

Some key points to make for speedy service as soon as the Interval starts.

- Use a hot water boiler instead of kettles to get a large quantity of water ready.

- Before the panto begins set all crockery out and pour milk into some cups.

- Make up the jugs of squash and water and set out plastic/paper cups. They are safer for children to use and need no washing up.

- Let the refreshment team know a time when they should start making tea. Base this time on experience gained during the Dress Rehearsal.

- Make sure cast orders for Interval refreshments are passed to the caterers.

- Make sure the cash float is in place with a designated volunteer ready to just take money.

At some time in the run up to the performance(s) the cast has been asked to place orders for refreshments to be served in their Changing Rooms during the panto interval. The catering staff needs to make up these orders and deliver them.

Remember: The panto cannot resume until every member of the audience who wants refreshment has received it and the crockery has been returned.

Unless washing up can be done well away from the performance area, it is best not to do it until the panto ends, as the noise can be very disturbing. No matter how quiet catering staff might say they can be, clearing away and washing up cannot be silent. It is amazing how intrusive the quietest sound can be.

'No poxy kitchen noise!'
[anon]

Act Eight – Scene Four: Bar

Does your venue have a licence to sell alcohol? If so, read on.

In the run up to the performance date(s) the people running the bar need to be given a firm idea of numbers. They also need a cash float. We find that red and white wine is as much as a bar needs to offer. Many supermarkets/wine merchants have a wine glass lending service if you get your wine from them. This service is usually free, with a charge only made for breakages – usually £1 per glass. If your venue has a fridge to chill the white wine, so much the better. If not, try to store this wine in home-based fridges until the last minute.

You might wish to open your bar as soon as the doors open, so giving your audience 30mins before the panto to have a drink. Don't be greedy with your pricing and keep it simple – for example, a standard £1.50 a glass. At this price you will sell your wine and your audience won't feel overcharged. As a bottle holds 6 glasses of wine, this should give you a healthy profit.

The bar needs a cash float with plenty of 50p coins (if you are charging £1.50 a glass).

Remember: The panto cannot resume until glasses have been returned and/or made safe.

As with crockery, washing up glasses is best left until after the panto ends.

Act Eight – Scene Five: Making Keepsakes

The panto makes loads of memories and everybody will have their own. But the production team might like to arrange for mementoes to be made on behalf of the cast and other major panto participants. This can take various forms:

1. The script: If you are making your own community panto, every one can have their own copy to keep.

2. Photographs: Arrange for a photographer (skilled amateur or local professional) to attend the Dress Rehearsal and take posed photos in full costume and make-up. We have been lucky having Jennie Banks, a professional photojournalist, taking our photos. She grew up in the village and her parents still live here.

3. Newspapers: Submit copies of your photos to a local newspaper accompanied by some copy for them to use. Or, arrange for an interview. Most local newspapers are hungry for stories, and although they will not usually (in our experience) publish an article/report prior to the performance, they are very happy to review/report afterwards. They are especially positive if you have provided them with a selection of well-taken, colourful photos in digital format. Check beforehand if they have specific technical requirements.

4. Film: Many people have digital film or video cameras. If you can get your hands on one, you can arrange for your performance to be filmed. In our experience film quality is better when the camera is in a static, fixed position, switched on and left to run. Attempts at panning or zooming may sound a good idea, but this often results in blurred, out of focus images and missed action.

Ensure that the camera has sufficient battery life. If you decide to use a mains lead as a power source, be careful with the cabling as if there is a chance for someone to trip over it, someone will. It is one of the facts of life.

5. Programmes: Cast can have free copies.

As a result of any/some/all of the above, panto mementoes are available when the show is over.

We put all the photographs taken at the Dress Rehearsal, and any others taken throughout the rehearsal period, on to a CD and give a copy to each family, which has participated in the panto. We put the filmed version on DVD and give a copy to each family too. Extra copies for grandparents and others carry a nominal charge of £2.

And you may be surprised how many people still like to see their names and faces in the local newspaper. Copies fly off the shelves as soon as word gets out: "We're in!"

"Robin Hood"
[Western Gazette, March 2013]

COLOURFUL CAST: The village of Drimpton presented Robin Hood at the village hall on the weekend. The pantomime which featured interlopers from other productions such as Snow White and the seven dwarves, has been described as a roaring success by organisers. *Pictures by Len Copland.*

Panto's merry men, women and children

BY SAM FORRESTER
e-mail newsdesk@westgaz.co.uk

DRIMPTON'S tenth family pantomime production has been described as a massive success by organisers.

The two performances of *Robin Hood* were well received by audiences in the village hall on Saturday afternoon and evening.

Andrew Pastor, who directed, produced and wrote the play said: "This was our tenth panto in 20 years and it was a roaring success.

"We had two full houses and with one of the shows we had an audience of mostly kids, so we could teach them about the rules of panto like shouting out 'he's behind you'.

"It was brilliant and for a village with a population of about 400 to generate that sort of response is great.

"We had a bit of an influx of people whose kids were involved in the production.

"About a year and a half ago after the last panto we did, three young people wanted to do *Robin Hood* so that's why we chose it.

"The essence of a Drimpton panto is that it's not your everyday version, so we threw in Snow White and the seven dwarves, a big bad wolf and the three little pigs.

"The cast ranges in age from 4 to 70 which I think is a rarity in this day and age.

"It is great to have adults and children working together.

> *The cast ranges in age from 4 to 70*

"It is often a challenge to find working adults who want to get involved and strut their stuff on stage, it often takes some encouragement.

"We do it for the fun although we do raise some funds which are divided between refurbishing the village hall kitchen and funding other productions."

HOW MANY?: Rosanna Marshall as Snow White with her 14 dwarf children from Drimpton, Broadwindsor and Burstock who make an appearance in Robin Hood.

"Dick Whittington"
[Western Gazette, April 2007]

MOTLEY CREW: The pirates of the Saucy Sal were in top swashbuckling form at the Drimpton pantomime Dick Whittington, directed and written by local man Andrew Pastor. Pictures by Jennie Banks.

CENTRE STAGE: Dick Whittington, front, with two other characters.

Rats run riot in popular pantomime

by **Gail Anderson**
Staff Reporter
e-mail crewkerne@westgaz.co.uk

CATS, rats, pirates and skeletons were among characters in a pantomime performed by the Drimpton Players.

Dick Whittington, written and directed by local man Andrew Pastor, attracted around 250 people to Drimpton Village Hall to watch the adventures of a horde of rats trying to take over the city of London from the mayor.

A variety of characters tried to lend a hand but, in the end, Penny Pumpernickel saved the day as she led the rats away with her magic pipe.

Netherhay resident Brian Heskerth, who played Captain Barnacle of the Saucy Sal, said the show was a real community effort. "It was a lot of fun to do and a lot of fun to be in," he said.

"There was wide involvement from across the community. We had around 35 people as cast members, and others helping out or doing the teas. Our youngest actor was six and one lady, who has been doing it every year for many years, is in her retirement.

"Anyone who wanted to have a part could go to the director; there were no special requirements."

Kate Heskerth, who also gave a hand with make-up and costumes, said: "Some people spent months getting their bits and pieces together, from the tails to the rats' ears. But it really was worth it, especially for the families and the young people.

"Children, who would normally just be going to school or playing on the computer, were turning up once a week every week for three months, three or four times a week towards the end.

"It really does bring families together, which does not happen very often these days."

● FOR more information on the Drimpton Players, call Andrew Pastor on 01308 868223.

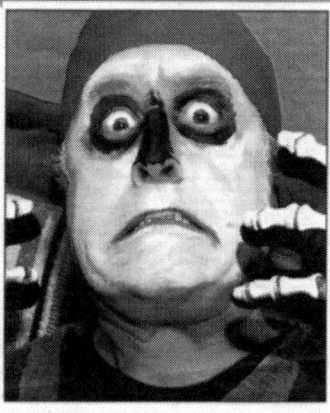

BONES MAN: Dave Crane puts in a bone-rattling performance as Skeleton Sam in the Drimpton pantomime Dick Whittington.

ACT NINE

SHOW TIME!

It is the day of our performance – a day of nervous excitement. Everyone is a bit hyper. Absolutely everyone. We are all wondering how we have come to be here. It is only a matter of weeks or a few months ago that we all started. At that time we were a lot of individuals coming together to make a panto happen. Then this moment seemed miles away and possibly not really considered at all. But here it is. Today! And we are a team. We have become friends. We are going to see it through together. Many of us are going into unknown territory. We all know we know what to do, but we can't help wondering what could happen if… if we forget our lines, if we drop our props, if the set change doesn't work, if the power fails. The list of 'ifs' is endless. We try and focus on the positives: Everybody in the audience is going to be cheering us on. Everyone in the cast looks great in their costumes. The set looks fantastic. The Director has told everyone to enjoy themselves, because if the cast is clearly having a good time, the audience will, too. And if the audience is clearly having a good time, they will cheer and boo and laugh at all the right times. And… so it goes on. The hours pass, but there are still a few to go. What is there that needs to be done?

So much has already been done in the run up and is in place. But there are things for the Director, Production Assistants and other Chiefs to do on the day.

- Check all aspects of the venue that will impact the performance are OK: all doors, toilets, seating, signage, heating, house lights.

- Set up the Box Office. Maybe this is only a table and chair by the main entrance.

- Ensure cash floats (in appropriate coinage) are available for people dealing with Box Office, programmes, refreshments and bar.

- Costume Chief checks costumes.

- Props Chief checks props.

- Director/Production Assistants check that the stage is set correctly.

- Sound Technician checks all sound equipment.

- Lighting Technician checks all stage lights and any emergency lights.

- Catering personnel set up kitchen and bar as this cannot be done during the performance.

- Production Assistants set up 'register' for cast to sign in on arrival at agreed time. This settles the nerves of the Director. That is a good thing.

- Put trust in everyone to do what they are responsible for.

On performance day, time moves at two distinct speeds. One speed is too slow. You just want to get the panto started! The other speed is much too fast. It can't be that time – I'm not ready! Time swings madly between the two. Across the village there are last minute activities. Cast members are searching for missing items of clothing, running through their lines again and again, stashing away some 'liquid refreshment' to see them through the trials ahead, trying to eat because they know they have to in spite of having no hunger at all. Children are being told to, "Stop jumping up and down. If you fall and break your leg, don't come running to me! It'd serve you right if you had to miss the panto!"

It's now an hour or so before the Curtain Goes Up and the first cast members arrive ...

They go to get ready as they did for the Dress Rehearsal, but today, once changed, they cannot leave their changing rooms after the doors have been opened to admit audience as we don't want the audience seeing any of the cast before their first entrances. As a result, the cast need to be occupied. For most people just sitting and waiting is not an option. Based on past experience this is what happens: The Men's Changing Room sets up its own bar with cans of beer and the telling of tall tales, while the Women's Changing Room is more decorous and embarks on a Drinks Party with banter and nibbles. Lubrication is a theme of community pantos. Leastways it is with us. Nobody drinks to excess (I think). If asked, they might say: "It's to settle nerves". The truth is that they are in party mood. The Children's Changing Room is (surprisingly?) more relaxed by comparison. In recent years visitors to their room discover them all with some piece of digital kit.

> 'We were well behaved `cos we had tablets and DS's. They are little Nintendo game things.'
> [Emily Chubb]

Or the children are chatting to the Production Assistant who is sitting with them (and eating sweets). They are the best-behaved members of cast, but don't go telling them that. Some worry a bit, but most are just looking forward to getting on stage and having fun!

Doors open 30 minutes before the performance is scheduled to start and audience start to enter the Hall. These people might have arrived by car. Have you dealt with potential car parking problems? Is anyone responsible for supervising parking and for making sure available space is used as effectively as possible? If you have limited car parking space, like us, as mentioned earlier, make sure that cast do not use it.

By the time doors open, the Box Office needs to be ready to operate. The great majority of the audience will have tickets in hand. These need to be checked. Some tickets are to be collected (and perhaps paid for). There might still be tickets for sale, so the Box Office Manager needs a cash float.

Front of House staff need to be ready in place before the doors open. They need to have programmes and their cash float.

Background Music (live or recorded) needs to be playing when the doors open.

The Bar needs to be ready to trade, if bar staff intend to open in the period before the panto begins. Have they got their cash float?

The minutes pass. The Hall fills with audience. Some hurry to grab what they feel are the best seats. Front of House staff are meeting, greeting and 'herding'. They have a maximum of 30 minutes to get everyone seated and settled and to sell programmes to those who would like one. The noise rises as people chat. This is not quiet like a real theatre; this is a social event.

The Director pays a final visit to the Changing Rooms to check that everyone is in place and ready. He/she definitely does not want to find a gap in the cast sign-in register at this late stage! In each room, (because it's not possible to have everyone together), I say something like: 'Well, everybody, there are only a few minutes before we start. We've got a great audience out there who are really looking forward to having a grand time. I know we're going to give them one. I want to thank you all for all your hard work over the weeks. The panto is now yours. Enjoy yourselves. Give it your all. You don't want to come off at the end feeling: "I really could have done better." Have lots of fun.'

Three minutes to go and counting. There are always late arrivals in the audience.

Beginners are in position in the wings or on stage, eager to get started.

> 'I remember the performance afternoon/nights themselves with us getting very excited about performing. We used to crack open the curtains to see if our family/friends had arrived and how full the audience was getting.'
> [Eleanor Dunhill]

We are approaching a tricky moment – getting messages to the Lighting and Sound Technicians and to Front of House that we are about to start. How you do it is determined by the geography of the venue and whatever technology you may have to hand. If you have walkie-talkies or mobile phones, use them. If you don't have viable technology, you need an agreed set of signals. For visual signals to work you need to be able to be seen and for people to be looking out for them. That doesn't always happen.

One minute to go. The doors are closed and background music fades out. The Box Office Manager needs to stay in place in case even now members of the audience turn up.

> 'There's always that minute before you start when you think: 'Oh, I've forgotten everything.'
> [Beryl Banks]

Signal to Front of House staff to switch off houselights.

Signal to the Sound Engineer to make sure all mics are on.

Signal to the Lighting Technician for the first cue to come up.

5..4..3..2..1..

It's CURTAIN UP on our PANTO!

The Curtains open to reveal our first brightly-lit colourful set immediately peopled with characters in whacky costumes. Within moments the audience has entered our panto world. The cast now takes them through the twists and turns of our story's plot, encouraging involvement every step of the way.

The first characters make their first exit. In the wings there is a wave of happiness, relief and pride. "We did it! It went well." "Did you hear the audience laugh?" "Too right, I did. Because we were good!" In our 2013 panto, 'Robin Hood', there was quite a lot of combined anxiety on stage in the first scene.

> 'It was the start so there was a responsibility to get things going. But it was a lovely feeling, being at the beginning, to have done it and then be able to sit and enjoy the rest of it.'
> [Lynwen Davies]

> 'Before I stepped through the door I was wanting to get on and get out there really. During rehearsals I was quite nervous during the early period. But by the end I was up for it. I did have a hip flask... I was very aware and appreciative that Andrew was behind the curtain in the first scene with the script just in case I fluffed up my lines.'
> [John Davies]

John was word perfect, proving that the old 'Bad Dress Rehearsal' adage is true!

Rehearsal time!

I have said elsewhere that the use of 'liquid refreshment' to lessen nerves is a given in our pantos over the years. This is, after all, a social occasion; our cast are not actors!

The panto rolls on. Baddies are boo-ed, much to their satisfaction. The youngest children are coo-ed over. Do they know they are cute? The Goodies get help from the audience who warn them of nasty goings on and cheer them when they make the Baddies look foolish. Scenes change. Curtains close, and sets are manhandled by cast members out of sight, while out front another scene plays. Curtains open again and we are in a different place entirely. We were in the forest, but now we are in a castle. Lighting changes. The sound effects come in on cue, many of them of bizarre invention. Actors reveal that they were 'naturals' after all, and some discover the delights of adlibbing – going off on creative tangents. The Director (if it's me) doesn't really relax. Whereas the children are totally unfazed by it all – they know what they are doing and do it well. They are at home on stage. They look forward to their next scene as soon as they have finished the previous one. The older children who are carrying so much of the panto on their shoulders are milking the audience like professionals. They demand to be watched, giving bravura performances.

There are nerves in the audience as well as on stage, especially among family members of the cast.

Some characters have to wait some time in their dressing rooms before making their first entrance.

> 'I have great memories of the 'dressing room' below the stage. The mad panic of people changing costumes with old pirate style chests on the floor with wigs and props spilling out of them, hairspray filling the room making you almost need a gas mask and all trying to do so as quietly as possible without disturbing the performance upstairs.'
> [Eleanor Dunhill]

The Three Little Pigs enjoyed a glass of bubbly to calm themselves and then took to the stage.

> 'We were all ready for action. We helped each other to put on costumes and make up and to be in the right place at the right time. The Three Pigs were ready for their first entrance and as we came on singing we received a huge laugh and round of applause. This helped us to "ham" it up even more.'
> [Leigh Carroll-Smith]

The blokes (who have tried not to show nerves because that's what blokes do) want to do well, and find that with the help of a few beers they are in fact doing really well. They seem surprised as much by that as by the fact that they come off after their scenes having had fun!

> 'To go up on stage and say words in a character is one thing, but to sing – as not being a singer – was different. But the chance to be a Lumberjack - it was the perfect character – If I was gonna do something on stage, it was perfect... We struggled in rehearsals as the four lumberjacks, but we all loved it. And it did everybody the world of good... I think the Lumberjacks gained 'blokey-ness'! It was only the normal characters of everyone that come through. We did a bit of singing. And we did it together. I started things off, but my mates were there... We were relaxed. You forgot you was up on stage... We all floated up and down.'
> [Mark House, Lumberjack]

The women are getting an equal amount of fun out of being naughty or silly, or both. All adults are rediscovering the joys of playing. Even those who have doubted themselves all along find the stage to be a happy place to be.

Within an hour or so we reach the Interval. The curtains close. There is an intake of breath and applause. Stage lights are dipped and Front of House staff switch on the houselights. Some windows may be opened to let in some air. The audience almost as one, get up (some more slowly than others), stretch their legs and burst into commentary about how well the panto's going. They never worried for a moment that it wouldn't! It is only to be expected that relatives focus on the performances of their children, grandchildren and parents, and are genuinely pleased with how well they've been doing. The pressure is now on the Refreshment and Bar staff to serve everyone as quickly as possible. In some pantos we have supplemented this staff with certain cast members who may have fulfilled their onstage role and are more than happy to be involved and help out. In the Changing Rooms scenes are being re-run by the cast, with a lot of "Did you see when…?" "What about when…?" and "The audience are good, aren't they?" "Do you think anyone noticed when I…?" They swoop on the refreshments, but aren't about to relax. It's a matter of taking a breather, nothing more. There is the second half still to do. The Director pops in on each Changing Room. If it's me, I say something like: 'It's going really well. The audience are loving it. Well done everybody. Now don't lose concentration. Keep the pace up and keep on having fun.'

In the Hall the queues for teas and wine gradually shorten. Catering staff begin to tidy up, collecting crockery and glasses, helped by Front of House staff, who are also responsible for checking that chairs aren't now blocking key entrance and exit routes. It is inevitable that rows will have become less precise. This needs dealing with to avoid any accidents during the fun and games of Part Two. As soon as the last tea is poured, the caterers stop serving, and Front of House staff begin encouraging the audience to return to their seats. This is where firm diplomacy can often be needed when conversations between members of the audience need to be brought to an end – quickly.

The audience has at last settled – or most of it has. The queue for the toilets is down to the last one or two.

The Director/Production Assistants tell the cast that it's three minutes to the start of Part Two and that Part Two Beginners need to get in position.

So we are approaching a repeat of the system that was in place before Part One, namely the checking with Front of House Staff, and the Technical Staff that everything is OK and the giving and receiving of signals.

5..4..3..2..1..

CURTAIN UP on Part Two!

The roller coaster ride begins again. The confidence created by Part One is clear on the faces and in the demeanour of cast members. But be prepared, if you have very young children in your cast they might run out of energy and need to sit out Part Two. Having a parent in the audience available as a refuge is a good idea.

In Part Two there is a greater deal of relaxation into the roles and possibly a bit more adlibbing than is really necessary. No problem.

But not everyone fully relaxes.

> 'Right through the performance there's always an undercurrent of tension and fear that you're going to let other cast members down and let the audience down by cutting a bit, or cutting someone's lines, or forgetting cues, or giving them the rough approximations of a cue! That is a worry that's always there – that you're going to mess up the Show for everyone else.'
> [Brian Hesketh]

And, of course, no matter how much you plan, the unexpected can happen. Props can malfunction.

> 'The memories of Widow Twankie in 'Aladdin and The Princesses' are with the Saturday afternoon performance when having the precarious job of hanging a washing line from one side of the stage to the other and then proceeding to hang various articles of laundry on the said line only to have the whole lot collapse around my ankles! Well I don't know how the audience handled the scene, but I suppose my only reaction was that "The show had to go on", as I proceeded to gather all the slightly soiled sheets, replacing the washing line and probably gibbering on and trying to ad-lib!'
> [Diane McCleod]

Photo: Widow Twankie with her man-eating mangle and the man-sized washing machine.

There can be costume mishaps, too. Ada the Laundry Maid in 'Mother Hubbard' back in 1998 was being played by Shirley Gibbs as a bulky woman in a large costume. She had already suffered the misfortune of having her nose pecked off (Ada, not Shirley) and was in a scene when she realized that she was getting a lot more laughs than she expected. However, this was not the result of her brilliant performance (on this occasion) but because Ada's voluminous knickers had dropped to her ankles. Like a true professional Shirley slipped them off and after a moment's thought tossed them into the wings. Cue more laughter.

If anything, Part Two of a panto is more manic than any Part One. It is the time when the plans of Baddies almost come to fruition, and when Goodies are pushed to the brink. All this accompanied by a refreshed audience sounding off – booing with gusto, cheering with the same. The "Oh, yes, you dids" and "Oh, no, you didn'ts" get ever louder. The "Behind yous" nearly raise the roof.

Family members in the audience – some having returned especially - are beaming or are bemused, or both.

> 'Coming back in university holidays to see Dad, the last standing Crane, on stage, not letting his forgotten lines and cues at all detract from getting into character.'
> [Rosie Crane]

The panto is now not merely chugging along; it is rushing headlong towards its climax. The chases get ever more energetic; there are people running everywhere. Excitement hits maximum. Waiting to come on gets harder.

> 'When we were entering the stage and the lumberjacks were there, they were going: "If you don't be quiet, we'll chop off your heads!!"'
> [Emily Chubb]

All the dwarfs kept their heads.

The audience at times don't know where to look as characters pop up all over the place. And then, with a twist, the Baddies overplay their hand and fail ignominiously. The Goodies have come through against all the odds. They and the audience cheer to the echo as the Baddies are dragged off for punishment, or, in the case of 'Robin Hood', as their meeting with the Wolf (off-stage) is reported. The Wolf has got severe in-die-gestion. This can only mean one thing... he's eaten something (or someone) Very Bad. Say no more! HOORAY!

And so we have reached the Happy Ending that everyone knew would come. The Boy has won the Girl. The Duke has kept his kingdom. Ali Baba is rightfully rich. The Old Woman Who Lived in A Shoe has a brand new shoe to call home. The Dame has got her beau. Ada the Maid has got her nose back. And every single Baddie has lost! HOORAY!

Blackout!

5..4..3..2..1..

Stage lights all come up in a blaze and it's time for the bows set against continuous applause. Faces beam on stage and out front. In fact, the Hall is full of smiles. On come the cast as choreographed in small groups, or in ones and twos, or, in the case of the youngest children, in a rush altogether. They know that they are the real stars! The Goodies are cheered. The Baddies (miraculously reprieved from jail or worse) are boo-ed. The audience realise this is their last chance to let rip.

And we have reached our destination – the End of Our Panto. There might have been a bit of choppy water during the show, but we've come though it all together; we haven't lost anyone overboard and to the audience it all has seemed like plain sailing. They have no idea!

Is this truly the end? Do you have a second performance? Later today? Tomorrow? Do you have more after that? If so, everything needs to be returned (each time) to as it was, in order for the whole thing to be done again (and again).

As I said much earlier we do two performances on the same day. So, immediately after our Matinee, costumes are taken off and re-hung, props are replaced ready for use, sets and scenery are put back as they need to be for the opening scene, chairs in the Hall are straightened up, odd cups and glasses are tracked down and all the washing-up is done, windows are opened to let the fug out and some fresh air in, litter is tidied up, the water boiler is re-filled, the toilets are checked to see if they pass muster for the evening audience (never run out of loo rolls!), cash is counted and floats re-calculated... and through it all, through all this purposeful busyness there is a constant commentary as every aspect of the performance, just finished, is re-lived.

Finally, the last volunteer is ushered out and the Hall is locked up. But not for long. In an hour or so we will all start returning to do it all again. And this time, we don't doubt that we can give our audience a great performance. Having done it once (and enjoyed it) we all plan to do it better and enjoy it even more!

When cast return, many of them are still wearing their Matinee make-up, which only needs retouching. All of them are still glowing from their earlier triumph with reports of what audience members have said. People have been receiving praise and the effect is electric. They are re-invigorated, bubbling with anticipation. There is nothing to worry about. There is no need for the Director to tell everyone to have fun (although I will). Nothing could stop them doing exactly that. I have a few words along the following lines: 'I know you're going to have a brilliant time and give your audience a great show. Just make sure you keep the concentration levels up. This is your last chance to show everyone just how good you all are. Oh, and by the way, you are planning to have fun, aren't you?' ... "Oh, yes, we are!"

And performance two swings into action along what – after one run – are now familiar lines.

The informal bar in the Men's Changing Room is getting lively. For Lumberjacks and Guards it's party time!

'It was the woodmen who instigated it, but it did spread. Some of the Baron's men got involved. And they all brought their own. It was very happy. The door was left open, and all we kept getting was 14 Dwarf children going by giving us dirty looks because they were in the next dressing room. They were very well behaved. The old adage "Don't act with animals and children". I think the children say: "Don't act with adults!" ... But James, of course, only had sherbet water!'
[Alan Clark, one of the Guards]

Photo: The Lumberjacks.

Cue James...

'Me and Jack walked into this changing room, sat down and looked at each other, wondering how it was gonna go. I think then Francis walked in with a beer. Other people walked in with multiple beers. Some people with bags of beer. This manly atmosphere with alcohol. A drink between men...as you do. But me and Jack being of the age we were (17 and 18), thinking: "This is great!" They came back

in the interval saying: "We better stay off this. We've gotta continue." And all the Lumberjacks are going: "YE-SSSS! We are Lumberjacks!!" And Brian sitting there going: "I shouldn't be doing this. I'm a wolf!" Certain people did drink more than others. But they did it all for a good cause. It helped. `Cos a lot of people in that dressing room hadn't done stage work before and it helped to ease the nerves a lot. And probably influenced how good they were in the pantomime. Fun times. By the end of the evening they were Lumberjacks! They weren't Francis and the rest; they were Lumberjacks!!'
[James Russ]

The Lumberjacks were definitely louder and considerably 'more relaxed'.

'It was easy for us because the pressure was off. If we'd've messed up nobody would've known. Like we did at the last bow. And then all of us were in fits of laughter and even at the very end we were all shaking with laughter.'
[Francis Medley]

A couple of hours after starting we reach the end. Well done to us all!

Photo: Taking bows at the end of 'Robin Hood'.

Clearly no community panto can finish with a curtain call and bows. There are the 'Thank Yous'. This is the time to mention names and say 'thank you' many times. But take care that people are not overlooked. Better to thank groups of people in general, than to mention individuals and then forget one.

So the thank yous are done and the stage empties of cast. But is this the end? Not if it's Drimpton, because now it's time to return to the normal world and have a party! We push back the chairs, bring out the food, crack open the drink and chat, while the youngest children slide on the floor and play games on the stage.

A great deal of well-deserved praise is given and received. Smiling is the order of the evening.

Finally, at a late hour, the lights are switched off as the last people leave, repeating a question that has been asked a lot since the panto ended: "What are we going to do next time?"

We've talked a lot about 'having fun', but has it been fun for everyone. What about the Reluctant Performer? Here is Melanie Russ, who was Bettina, one of The Three Little Pigs in 'Robin Hood'.

> 'I'd never done that kind of thing. Not confident. Shy of putting myself in the spotlight. It went against a lot of my natural instincts. So I had to push myself forward to do it. I am the reluctant performer. For a lot of the time in rehearsals I was thinking: "How did I get myself on this side of the curtain? Why am I here and not backstage? I don't do this. I'm normally in the supporting role." It was a tables-turned situation.'

Did you feel like backing out?

> 'Yes! Frequently. Right up to the last minute. But then I realised I'd be letting an awful lot of people down if I did back out. I thought, I can't take this "I did it once" to a conclusion, if I do back out.'

How were you that moment before going on stage?

> 'Jelly. There was a moment I was not sure my legs would carry me onto the stage. I was terrified; worried that I was going to forget my lines, that I wouldn't be able to adlib if I forgot my lines, that I'd be completely tongue-tied, physically rooted to the spot.'

And having got on?

> 'I wouldn't say I was aware of time passing – consciously thinking this is an eternity. The main feeling was: "Phew! We've got that scene carried off. On to the next one. Let's hope we can keep this going all the way through!"'

Any enjoyment?

> 'It wasn't totally suffering. I enjoyed the camaraderie, the rehearsals and the social side of it. Getting to know people

in the village I would not have necessarily interacted with. So that was very good, but the actual going on stage and performing in front of an audience was the bit I could live without. I didn't find a part of me that had not been awakened before!'

Parents spend a lot of time and energy supporting their children. Are roles ever reversed? Are children impressed, understanding, encouraging?

'It was quite funny to watch her, because she'd never do anything like that at home. I never thought in a million years that she'd be in a pantomime – that sort of role. She always says that when she was young she was always part of the chorus, never got a line or anything. But she did it. Yeah! It was weird. She was terrified. I remember on the performance she was: "Oh my God. I don't think I can go on. I can't do it." I was, "Pull yourself together, woman!" ' [Emily Russ, Melanie's daughter]

Like Melanie said, she did it once. She proved to herself and to her family that she could do it.

The performances are over, but our panto isn't quite done and dusted yet. Everything has to be dismantled, sorted, tidied, cleared away, cleaned up, returned, disposed of.

ACT TEN

Including: Goodbye. Set, Scenery and Props. Costumes.

Act Ten: Goodbye

The next day, usually a Sunday, during the morning, a group of stalwart volunteers turn up – some feeling a bit under the weather. These are real troupers.

> 'I always tried to get there the following morning to clear up, to have a laugh about how it went and the bits we missed. The lingering feeling...'
> [Dave Crane]

Within a short time, two or three hours only, it is as if the panto had never been. The effect is not unlike that when all the Christmas decorations, which have been up for a few weeks, are taken down. The normal space returns, looking bare and a bit dull.

Everything that has been borrowed is neatly piled up ready for the owners to reclaim it. As for the rest there are hard decisions to make. Of the things that you have made what do you keep and what do you get rid of? Though I suppose the first question you need to ask yourselves is: "Will we be doing another panto in the near future?" If the answer is 'no', the solution is straightforward. Give or throw away the lot. Harsh, but that is how it is.

Let us ask the same key question again: "Will we be doing another panto in the near future?" This time the answer is a resounding 'Yes'! Now what do you do? If you have unlimited storage space to hand (at the venue or elsewhere) I suppose you could keep everything. But that is unlikely. The decisions you are faced with are hard, as I said before, because a whole range of volunteers have given their time, energy and skill to make it all. And now some of it has to be thrown out.

Act Ten – Scene One: Set, Scenery and Props

First, the big stuff – the backdrops, large sets and pieces of scenery.

Backdrops, Sets and Scenery:

Once made or acquired, backdrops must be kept. They can be repainted, re-hung and re-used time and time again.

If you have made sets and scenery flatpack-style in sections that fold or can be separated, they could be stored flat against a wall, maybe. Like the backdrops they can be repainted and used again and again, especially if they have been made to fit the venue that you are likely to use again. To give you an example, several years ago our set constructors built a pair of simple, large, rectangular screens out of battens covered with thick cardboard. One screen had a working door set in as part of it. The other was a wall with a cut-out window in it. The two were then hinged together so that they could stand on the stage like an open book. Are you with me?

📷 Photo: Painting part of the cottage.

📷 Photo: The finished cottage on stage.

In the panto the screens were made for they became the outside of a cottage in a few scenes. Stood the other way round they became the inside of the same cottage in some other scenes. It was so useful that at the end we undid the hinges and kept them. Since then they have been resurrected and used in two other pantos to date (- cottages appear in so many panto stories, as seen earlier). That is just one example. So, before you break up and throw away pieces of set, think.

However, there are always going to be some items, like The Old Woman Who Lived In A Shoe's shoe, that worked wonderfully, looked fantastic, but can never be anything other than T. O. W. W. L. I. A. S.'s shoe, so it had to go.

Smaller pieces of set:

Most of these can be discarded if storage is a problem. But there are some basic items which we keep, chief among them being steps and blocks, both of which are always useful. Steps and blocks can be sat or stood on and so give the potential for different levels on stage and can move wherever needed. They are also made robustly out of wood and unlike the sets demand more time, cost and effort should you need to remake them for a future panto.

(Unborrowed) Props:

There are two categories. Ones you have made. Ones you have bought. Almost all are panto-specific. Are they ever going to be re-used? You had a gang of pirates and each one had a cutlass made of plywood; do you think you might need them again? If you are a natural hoarder, of course you will want to keep them. If you are a minimalist, they'll be chucked away without a second thought.

But some props are thrown away with a heavy heart – the man-eating mangle made for Widow Twankie had to go, but not until many of us had had a last trip through its rollers!

What I can say for sure is that each time we keep stuff only to find it and throw it away a few years later. Make of that what you will.

It's even harder to throw away props you have bought. They've only been used a handful of times after all. We never spend a lot on props, so, if we don't want to keep them, rather than put them in the bin, we tend to share them among cast members who might want them. At least this way they get more use and our 'green' consciences are eased.

Act Ten – Scene Two: Costumes

This is the hardest area in which to make decisions. Costumes are essentially personal; they have been made by someone for someone else. Throwing them away or taking them to the clothing bank can be seen as being insulting to the maker. But think hard; whatever you decide to keep needs to be stored in such a way as to be usable and accessible in a year's time or longer. And finding such a store can be difficult or near impossible.

You need a safe, dry space. This could be a house loft. But if so, there is the matter of access and being dependent on goodwill. It could be a community storeroom. Again there is the matter of access - and keys, as the store needs to be lockable. Do not use any storage space that is prone to cold and damp: your costumes will go musty, mouldy and become un-wearable quite quickly.

Let's say you have a suitable safe, dry, accessible space. Before storing anything there you need dress rails, hangers, large polythene covers as used by dry-cleaners, and large plastic lidded stackable storage boxes for items that cannot be hung up.

Now you have to decide what to keep. How? The rules that apply for sets and props apply equally to costumes. Do you see them being used again, with or without minor modifications? You do? Then you keep them. Cover the hang-able items before hanging them on the dress rails. Sort the un-hangables into categories before putting them into the storage boxes, which you label before you forget what's inside. There is no way you will remember what is where next time you need something.

Before discarding costumes retrieve any elements that could be re-used – buttons, zips, collars, belts, trimming and put them in a drapery box. Even then, before binning the costume, ask yourself if it or any part of it should go into the 'materials bag' – the bag to hold oddments for use by future costume-makers.

ACT ELEVEN

And finally ...

Having cleared up, tidied away or discarded all the paraphernalia of your panto, what is there left to do?

- Make sure all cast and backstage crew have their copies of whatever keepsakes you have decided upon, eg: film on DVD, photos on CD, programme, etc.

- Make sure everyone's expenses are accounted for.

- Tell the community how much money the panto has raised, both in total and then after all deductions.

- Have the happy task of deciding what to do with the profits!

Panto is never ever completely put away. Its echoes re-echo. Children grow up. They become involved in the serious stuff of life. But panto has the knack of popping up unexpectedly.

> 'At my wedding reception in 2013, in Broadwindsor Village Hall, someone in the know shouted out: "It's panto season!" when Dad stood up to make his 'father of the bride' speech (granted he had just beaten a gong to get the guests' attention).'
> [Rosie Crane]

Not Quite Finished...

During the process of collecting the thoughts, memories and anecdotes of panto participants I interviewed the Rawlings Family – Richard and Sue, with their sons, Harry and Alfy. In 'Robin Hood' Richard was Sid, one of the Lumberjacks; Sue was Mrs Ditchwater, one of the Market Traders; Harry was Trickster and Alfy was Shouter, two of the 14 Dwarfs. Here is what they said, as they said it, which I think echoes so much of what has been said above.

Do you remember the 'Grand Old Duke of York' in 2011?

Alfy:
Only that we had to go up the Hill!

AP:
What was the best bit in 'Robin Hood' last year?

Harry:
Chasing parents around the room!

Sue:
For me it was nerve wracking to start with. My favourite bit was the night. When I was actually on the stage, the feeling was fantastic! But right up to then it was awful! The feeling I got from the actual night was great.

Richard:
We did the afternoon one and then in the evening one there was more buzz. We did more in our voice, in everything.

Sue:
I think by that time I thought: "Oh I can do this." I realised I wasn't as bad as I thought I was!

Richard:
We could really get away with it!

Sue:
At the very beginning when I agreed I thought: "Something's gone wrong here. How can I get out of it?"

Richard:
But we got into a good routine, really. Every Tuesday or Friday – it went quite well. When it stopped it left a big hole in our life. When we finished it was really a bit dull. Nothing to look forward to.

Sue:
But for that week afterwards we were still buzzing from the time. It was in the paper. We've all talked about it, but it's finished now.

AP:
Why didn't you say 'no'?

Sue:
Well...for the children. It was nice to do it as a family together.

Richard:
We like to do things as a family.

AP:
How did you feel when you entered for the first time?

Sue:
I was all right in the afternoon one. We knew our parents were there. But we didn't know of anybody that we knew there. In the evening it was worse; there were all Richard's friends there. As I came out I saw them! That was the most nerve wracking bit, thinking, "Oh, my God, what are they gonna think of me?"

Richard:
It's like going on a fair ride for the first time – doing something daredevil. You know what I mean? You get like an adrenalin rush.

Sue:
I never thought I would do it. Never ever did. I surprised myself. Jo House and her family thought the same. We surprised ourselves.

Richard:
I remember coming off and thinking: "Wow, that was good." We never ever done anything at school. It's only because of our boys – we wanted to be a part of their life. They were in it, so why not. To do more with them.

Alfy:
I thought they were a bit silly, but they meant to be silly.

Sue:
What about my singing?

Alfy:
A bit horrible.

Sue:
I can't sing, but I did it in front of all those people. I thought

I'd never ever sing on stage, but in the end I didn't mind. Like you said when we were doing it – the more silly you are, the less people will notice if it's not good. The more embarrassed you look, the more they'll notice you.

AP:
What was it like in the Men's Changing Room?

Richard:
Yeah!! We were relaxed.

Sue:
Calming their nerves.

Alfy:
Drunk!

Richard:
It was party time.

Harry:
They were making a racket!

Richard:
And we could hear you lot!

AP:
What was the best thing for you?

Sue:
The evening. So much better than the afternoon. The shock of how good it could be. I was nervous rehearsing, but I was building up to a panic. And when I actually did it, I really surprised myself. Because I thought I'd be nervous and forget my lines, but I didn't. I was amazed how good it was. And in the evening there was much more atmosphere. Absolutely fantastic.

AP:
And the best thing for you?

Richard:
I think all of it. Even the rehearsals. We got there in the end. I was obviously rehearsing at work as well, you know. People were looking at me, but I didn't really care, like. I was in the

middle of a field, singing. You know what I mean? Me singing "I'm a Lumberjack..." Them thinking: "What's he on?" And going down Danny's helped a lot. Definitely. Singing the song.

Sue:
I rehearsed when I had to and then lived normal life. You had pantomime and normal life. I didn't mix the two. I didn't get myself into the part, I don't think, until the night, really. Then I let rip.

Richard:
Panto brought all the villagers together. All of it for me was enjoyable. And the way it went.

Sue:
I think it's nice also to see other people rehearsing. And when they are forgetting their lines, it makes them human and you feel better. Even ones who've done it for years and years will forget things.

Richard:
I actually went into a shop in Crewkerne – Mrs Hill was in there – We were looking at 'The Western Gazette' – at the photos. Yes, I was a Lumberjack! Brilliant! People I bumped into in the shop saw me.

Sue:
At the end people in the audience were saying "It was really good" and how good everybody was – it made us feel like backstage after a film – like real actors would feel. It made us feel really, really good.

Richard:
I think doing things like panto is a learning curve for the boys. It makes them more confident.

Sue:
And it makes a connection between all the children in the village. Not just the younger ones, but the older children, too. Now they'll see them on the street and know them.

Richard:
It gives all four of us a chance to learn stuff.

It's all there:

- The Fun
- The Nerves
- The Buzz
- The Growing Confidence and Self-Belief
- Being Together
- Family and Friends
- The Sense of Achievement
- The Applause

Exit Lines:

Here are other people reminiscing.

'Like my sister, Eleanor, I can remember the bustle of the dressing rooms. The Village Hall as the Pantomime venue seemed so big back then. The dressing room was a maze of people, and the stage itself was vast, with enough room for stage props and for a few of us to hover in the wings. On stage, the audience seemed huge and scary! Now when I go past the Hall, it strikes me how tiny it now appears.

What strikes me now is the real sense of Community. I always had a real sense of warmth when I considered the people I was acting with - Everyone was so familiar.'
[Zacyntha Dunhill]

'Attending the last panto, 'Robin Hood', with Lizzie and Mum and Lizzie's baby Niamh. John Horne absolutely nailing the Sheriff. Seeing new little Drimpton dwarves, Ella Horne as the commanding Red Riding Hood when I remember the day she was born as clearly as yesterday, and marvelling at the swift passage of time. And yet the panto doesn't change. Dad, demoted to a supporting role due to lack of time/memory to learn scripts, hugely over-compensating for this by attempting to steal the limelight in any scene despite not having any lines.'
[Rosie Crane]

'Memories of panto days and growing up in the village I always will have a great recollection of my childhood being full of laughter and "He's behind you!" moments.'
[Eleanor Dunhill]

'The whole thing about the pantos was the involvement of so many people in the village, all working together, such a community thing. All the back-stage and support people who took care of the refreshments, the kitchen, the costumes, the props, the scenery, all of which recycled in

new lives I don't know how many times. Over the years, the then-children grew up, becoming parents to the next gaggle of dwarves and elves and, sadly, one or two older ones disappeared from the cast and audience, but there was always the sense of it moving on, a kind of cycle.'
[Dave Crane]

'I was so glad that I did join in. Watching the family do rehearsals and do the pantomime as well, if I hadn't've put me hand up, it would've been one of those cases where you thought: "I should've done that." Then, `cos we did do it... well, the atmosphere, that elation when the panto was over, people were beaming, flowing over with fun.'
[Mark House]

'When it all finishes, it's sad really.'
[Robert Fooks]

'We would be a lesser village without panto.'
[Kate Hesketh]

'It was fun.'
[Matthew Medley]

How We Have Made Community Pantos

This has been not so much a 'How To Make Community Pantos' book, more a 'How We Have Made Community Pantos' book. What we have told you about is what has worked for us. If you fancy doing your own panto, it is for you to pick and choose based on the community you belong to and all it can offer. Believe me, over the years we have made our fair share of wrong choices and bad decisions. As a result we have wasted time and energy and sometimes money. But then again we were discovering 'How to…' as we went along. And had a lot of fun in the process. Often we had no idea that we had done the right thing in the right way until afterwards when the applause was ringing in our ears.

Photo: The Cast of 'Robin Hood', 2013.

Cue the Final Curtain

The End

Appendix I - People

On Stage

Members of Panto Casts 1993 to 2013:
Baker, Hilary
Baker, Lee
Baker, Louise
Baker, Mike
Banks, Beryl
Banks, Jennie
Beck, Tom
Beck, Will
Beckingham, Iris
Beckingham, Maya
Beckingham, Sage
Beckingham, Tamsyn
Bellorini, Grace
Bellorini, Rosa
Bracher, Rod
Broom, Johnathan
Broom, Pat
Bryant, Olivia
Carroll-Smith, Leigh
Carter, Teresa
Chubb, Emily
Chubb, Isobel
Clark, Alan
Clegg, David
Clegg, Ellen
Clegg, John
Comben, Art
Corbett, Caitlin
Corbett, Nina
Couch, Lucy
Crane, Dave
Crane, Lizzie
Crane, Oliver
Crane, Richard
Crane, Rosie

Crine, Beccy
Davies, Hannah
Davies, John
Davies, Lynwen
Davies, Sian
Dawson, Grace
Dodge, Sue
Down, Dickie
Downs, Samantha
Dunhill, Eleanor
Dunhill, Zacyntha
Dunton-Rose, Jessamie
Dunton-Rose, Justine
Edmunds, Jennie
Edwards, Keith
Elliott, Emily
Emmerson, Josie
Fogg, Amanda
Fogg, Chris
Fogg, Tim
Fooks, Ellie
Fooks, Robert
Fooks, William
Fowler, Danielle
Fowler, Kieron
Gerrard, Eddie
Gibbons, Alex
Gibbs, Amy
Gibbs, Cliff
Gibbs, Emily
Gibbs, Molly
Gibbs, Shirley
Gibbs, Tom
Grainger, Jim
Guppy, Annie
Hedditch, Georgia
Hedditch, Rebecca
Hesketh, Brian
Hesketh, Kate
Holt, Natalie

Hooker, Sandra
Horne, Anne
Horne, Ella
Horne, Joe
Horne, John
Horne, Katie
Horne, Michelle
House, Amy
House, Jack
House, Jo
House, Mark
Hunt, Katie
Hyde, Lottie
Kirk, Danny
Lock, Abigail
Macleod, Bob
Macleod, Diane
Mansfield, Jodie
Mansfield, Sadie
Marriage, Holly
Marriage, Jack
Marshall, Charlotte
Marshall, Rosie
Martin, Anya
Martin, Guy
Meaden, Jessica
Medley, Francis
Medley, Matthew
Molony, Jo
Newman, Mel
Pastor, Andrew
Pearce, Abigail
Porteous, Eleanor
Porteous, Kay
Rawlings, Alfy
Rawlings, Harry
Rawlings, Richard
Rawlings, Sue
Reeves, Rosie
Rogers, Brett

Russ, Emily
Russ, James
Russ, Melanie
Russ, Verity
Shepherd, Bob
Shepherd, Frank
Shute, Andy
Shute, Nicki
Sibley, Corben
Sibley, Ryan
Singleton, Hannah
Singleton, Joe
Singleton, Josh
Smith, Mike
Trott, Mary
Trott, Sam
Trowbridge, Ellie
Tubb, Adam
Tubb, Nick
Turnbull, Nathan
Waterman, Dan
Waterman, Sophie
Watts, Jean
Watts, Viv
Wiles, Sophie
Woodbury, Gemma

Backstage

Members of the cast often had a range of backstage roles as well, whilst other people applied all their efforts backstage, and they appear below:
Adam, Jock
Adams, Neville
Akerman, Gill
Anderson, Judith
Baker, Doris
Baker, Karen
Baker, Mark
Baker, Roy

Banks, Ken
Beck, Jenny
Benveniste, Pip
Blogg, Maurice
Bowen, Carol
Brookes, Tristan
Bryant, Tina
Clark, Janice
Cubbage, Gwen
Curtis, Clair
Desmond, Francis
Dodge, Des
Down, Su
Featherstone, Jim
Flood, Maureen
Fry, Janet
Gibbons, Tony
Goble, Tessa
Gray, Bob
Gray, Joyce
Halter, Aviva
Harding, Ken
Harris, Ann
Heal, Richard
Hill, Dennis
Hill, Gwen
Hill, Hazel
Hill, Ron
Holt, Kim
Huband, Peggy
Hyde, Ann
Hyde, Phil
Jelfs, Peter
Jenkins, Barbara
Jones, Ann
Kirkwood, Gloria
Leake, David
Leake, Diana
Lock, John
Marsden, Jane

Marsden, Norman
Marshall, Duncan
Marshall, Zoe
Medley, Joanna
New, Marianne
Sach, Stan
Saunders, Carol
Saunders, Mike
Shepherd, Rosemary
Smith, Linda
Smith, Roger
Taylor, Kath
Teasdale, Toby
Teasdale, Tom
Thomas, Roger
Thomas, Viv
Toogood, Ann
Toogood, Geoff
Warner, Jean
Warner, Jim
Wheeler, Graham
Williams, Kathy
Winn, Jeanette
Woodbury, Sue
Wright, Barbara
Wright, John
Yates-Jones, Hazel
Young, Deirdre

It has taken a grand total of 219 people plus untold others over 20 years to make 10 village pantos.

Appendix II - Stage Extension Pictures

1. Stage Extension folded down.

2. Removing the sectional beam that fills the gap above the hinges.

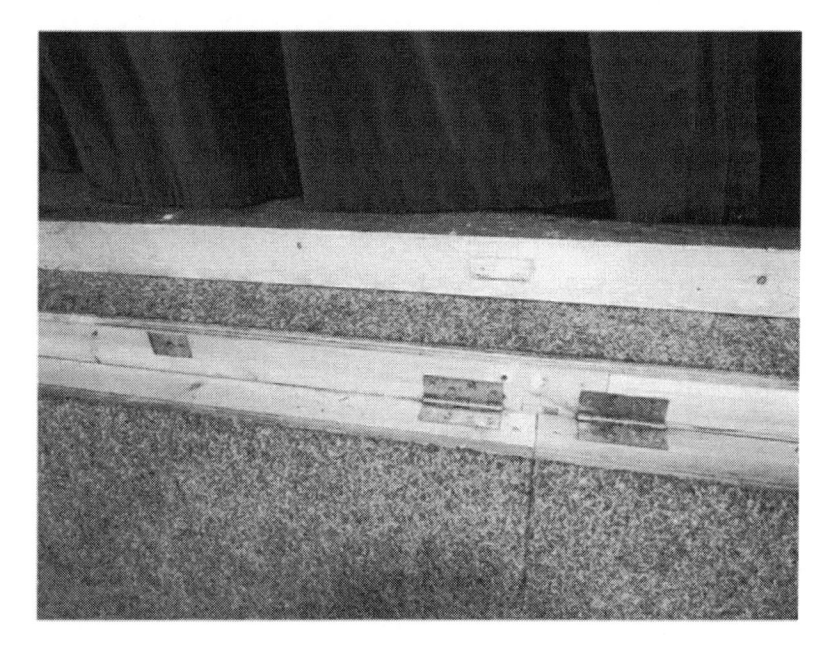

3. Lifting one half of the extension, revealing the legs folded back against the wall.

4. Pulling out the legs. Fixing them to the floor with drop bolts.

5. After raising and securing the second half of the extension, fixing the curtain 'skirt' in place with Velcro.

6. The stage extension in place, providing an extra 1m 20cm in stage depth.

Appendix III - Sound and Lighting Plot

LIGHTS: Bring up 1-7 SOUND: Forest backing track ON SOUND: FADE Forest backing track LIGHTS: Spot on TREE SOUND: WOLF ominous entry LIGHTS: OFF spot on TREE LIGHTS: ON 10-11 for DWARF entry SOUND: Several bumps followed by comic crash LIGHTS: OFF 10-11	[CURTAINS OPENING] ACT 1 SCENE 2: In Sherwood Forest. [SNOW WHITE emerges from behind tree. She's been picking flowers.] SNOW: [to audience] Oh, hello. Fancy seeing you here in Sherwood Forest. I'm Snow White. Pleased to meet you. All of you. [She curtseys] You haven't seen the dwarfs have you? **Seven of them?** No? Good. That means I can have a bit of me-time. People say the forest is beautifully peaceful, but the dwarfs are always 'hey-ing' and 'ho-ing' like dwarfs do. It can get on a girl's nerves. [**WOLF emerges** from behind a tree] But here in this glade a girl can be on her own and think nice thoughts. And do you know what I'm thinking? Do you? [pause] I'm thinking I'm not alone. There's you of course, but I have a feeling there's someone else. [Behind you business] Have you seen something? What? A Wolf? Are you sure? Are you really sure? Are you really, really sure? Are you really, really, really sure? [Adlib scene, taking and misinterpreting directions from audience until, just as WOLF is about to get SNOW without her knowing...] DWARFS: (voices offstage) **Snow White? Where are you?** [WOLF sneaks off.] SNOW: [to audience] You were teasing me about the wolf, weren't you? It was only the dwarfs, wasn't it? [AUDIENCE: No!] Oh, yes it was! AUDIENCE: Oh, no it wasn't. SNOW: Oh, yes it was. [etc] Look, we are going to be friends, aren't we? So let's not argue. DWARFS: [Offstage] Snow White? Snow White? SNOW: [reluctantly calling] I'm over here. DWARFS rush on from several places **and bump into each other ending in a heap.** SCUTTLER: There you are. CLUTTER: I saw her first. TRICKSTER: I saw her way before you did. I saw her from miles away. ALGIE: Excuse me. I think you will find that we all saw her at exactly the same time. [With SNOW's help DWARFS begin to sort themselves out.] SCUTTLER: [to ALGIE] Why can't you talk normal? ALGIE: (correcting) Normally. PICKLER: Like what we do. ALGIE: (correcting) Like us. WHISTLER: Stop doing that! ALGIE: What? HATTER: Just cos you lived in the palace cellars before you came to Sherwood Forest, you think you're so posh. ALGIE: We cannot all be lucky enough to have lived with the pigs on Mother Hubbard's farm. SHOUTER: (angry) There's nothing wrong with pigs. ALGIE: Nothing at all. Some of my friends are pigs. SNOW: [interrupting] Dwarfs! Dwarfs! Behave yourselves. Haven't you noticed? We are not alone. [DWARFS take time before they notice audience. **When they do they panic and try to hide.**]

	SNOW:	I don't believe there is a wolf.
	DWARFS:	[shocked] What?!
	SNOW:	Sometimes I wish there was a Big, Bad Wolf, so I could be rescued from it by a….
	SCUTTLER:	By a what?
SOUND: Short Romantic theme LIGHTS: Brief Pink Spot! [NOTE: This sound made live with coconut shells.] LIGHTS: ON 10-11	SNOW:	**You know…a hero! Tall, dark and handsome.** Or failing that, short, pale and spotty. Someone. Anyone. It's about time something exciting happened in my life. Life here is so boring! I want an adventure! (**SOUND** of horses approaching OFF at back of Hall.) What's that?
	CLUTTER:	Sounds like the Sheriff.
	SNOW:	What's he doing coming this far into the forest? Do you think the evil Queen has sent him to track me down?
	ALGIE:	Ever since that magic mirror told her you were the most beautiful girl in the land she's had it in for you.
	SNOW:	It's not fair!
	TRICKSTER:	Don't worry, Snow White. The Sheriff's a rubbish hunter.
	WHISTLER:	He never catches anything.
	PICKLER:	He couldn't catch a cold in a freezer.
	HATTER:	Or a pasty in a pie shop.
	SCUTTLER:	Or a jelly in the face at a Youth Club party.
	SNOW:	OK. OK. I get it. But I don't want this to be his lucky day. I'd better be off. (SNOW exits, to audience) You won't tell the Sheriff you've seen me, will you? Promise? Thank you.
	ALGIE:	(listening to hooves.) The Sheriff's showing off as usual.
	PICKLER:	Pretending he's got a horse.
	SCUTTLER:	When he's just banging a pair of coconut shells together.
SOUND: Groan	TRICKSTER:	Doing his nut as always. (pause) Geddit? Doing his **nut!**
	SCUTTLER:	(about audience) Quality material is wasted on this lot.
	ALGIE:	This script isn't exactly quality material though, is it? [DWARFS agree.]
	SHER:	(From Hall) Whoa, boy. Whoa? (SHER, LADY & GUARDS whinny)
	SCUTTLER:	We'd better look busy.
SOUND: Evil entrance SOUND: End evil entrance LIGHTS: OFF 10-11	ALL DWARFS:	(start singing) 'Hey ho. Hey ho. **It's off to work we go….**
	SHER:	(interrupting, entering, singing) 'Boo me, Hiss me. Just to show you miss me. As long as you hate me, it's all **right!**' [switching, stopping DWARFS exit] Just hold it there you blundering bunch of dodgy dwarfs.
	LADY:	Where do you think you're all going?
	ALGIE:	(very friendly) Good morning, Sheriff, Ma'am. We're off to work. I must say, you're both looking…. er…spiffing.
	GLIMMER:	A visit from you makes our day, doesn't it? [DWARFS agree.]
	LADY:	We make your day, do we?
	SHER:	Well, my itty bitty, teeny-weeny tree huggers, we're here to make your day extra super specially special, (to GUARDS) aren't we, men?
	'ERB:	Extra
	'ARO:	Super
	'ENR:	Specially
	'ORA:	Special

LIGHTS: Flicker 1-7 LIGHTS: Stop Flicker 1-7	SNOW:	[encouraging DWARFS] Come on. **Don't be scared**. [to AUDIENCE] You're friendly, aren't you? [to DWARFS] Now, introduce yourselves.
	SCUTTLER:	Do we have to?
	SNOW:	Yes, you do.
	SCUTTLER:	I'm Scuttler. [to TRICKSTER] Now you!
	TRICKSTER:	I'm Trickster.
	[The other DWARFS introduce themselves in the same way. ALGIE is last.]	
	ALGIE:	And I'm Algernon Arbuthnot. But friends call me Algie.
	SNOW:	That's better. You don't want them [signals AUDIENCE] thinking you're weedy, do you? Dwarfs must be brave. You must be bold. You must be ….[runs out of ideas]
	HATTER:	Beardless!
	CLUTTER:	Bald!
	PICKLER:	Brainy!
	GLIMMER:	Bright, bonny and beautiful!
	SNOW:	But remember. There is nothing like a dwarf!
	SONG:	[led by STRINGER] There is nothing like a dwarf. Nothing in the wood. From east to west, from south to north, There is no-othing like a dwarf. Nothing tracks like a dwarf. [DWARFS mime tracking] Or attacks like a dwarf. [DWARFS mime attacking] Nothing hides like a dwarf [DWARFS mime hiding] Or decides like a dwarf [DWARFS mime thinking] Nothing eats like a dwarf. [DWARFS mime eating] Or repeats like a dwarf. [DWARFS belch!] There is really, truly - Everybody must agree - No-thing… like… a…. dwarf!
SOUND: Cheering & Applause	SNOW:	Where's your get-up and go?
	TRICKSTER:	Got up and gone!
	SNOW:	Your derring-do?
	WHISTLER:	Derring done!
	SNOW:	I give up! One of these days you're going to have to stand up and be counted [DWARFS immediately stand to attention and count themselves off from 1 to 7, when SNOW interrupts.]
	SNOW:	What are you doing?
	SCUTTLER:	Standing up to be counted….. Now where were we?
	[DWARFS start counting from 1 to 7 again, beginning with the 8th DWARF….They finish.]	
	SNOW:	But there's more than seven of you.
	GLIMMER:	Rubbish. There's always seven of us.
	STRINGER:	Everybody knows that.
	GLIMMER:	I mean, whoever's heard of Snow White and the 8 dwarfs?
	STRINGER:	Or 9?
	GLIMMER:	Or 10?
	STRINGER:	Or more!
	SNOW:	Oh, what's the point? I'm going. [moves to exit.]
SOUND: Ominous Da-da-da-dah! LIGHTS: Flicker 1-7	SCUTTLER:	Mind you don't bump into…. **The Wolf!** [ALL DWARFS react.]
	CLUTTER:	He's wicked.
	HATTER:	And not in a good, well-wicked way.

	ALL GUARDS: Yes, Sire!
	SHER: (to audience) You can't beat a good yes-man.
	'ERB: 'Scuse me, Sire, but you can.
	SHER: Can what?
	'ERB: Beat a good yes-man.
	'ARO: (bragging) Yes, Sire. Yesterday you beat me and 'Orace and 'Erbert....
	SHER: Look, that's not what...
	'ENR: (upset) And you promised you'd beat me, too, Sire, but you never got round to it.
SOUND: Thwack!	SHER: That can be remedied! **[SHERIFF hits him]**
	'ENR: (happy) Oh, thank you, Sire.
	LADY: (to DWARFS & AUDIENCE) Now, you meddling midgets and you local layabouts, stop picking your noses and listen, my lovey-dovey hubby has a cunning plan.
	ALL GUARDS: A very cunning plan.
	SHER: A plan to make loads of lolly,
	LADY: Mountains of money.
	SHER: Great dollops of dosh – (explaining) We are going to be..... rich!
	LADY: Ooh. The very idea gives me goose bumps!
	'ERB: But, Sire, you already <u>are</u> rich.
	SHER: How true. How very true.
	LADY: Dearest, you should've said we're going to be rich–er! Much, much richer!
	SHER: Take a good look around you. What do you see? Something beginning with T.
	'ORA: Oo, ooh! I love a game of I-Spy!
	[GUARDS spend a lot of time thinking.]
	SHER: [gives clues] We are in a forest... Sherwood Forest...
	'ERB: Toothpaste.
	'ORA: Telescope.
	'ARO: Teapot.
	'ENR: I know!.... Teddy bear!
	'ERB, 'ARO, 'ORA: (eager) Where? Where?
SOUND: Multiple Thwacks!	SHER: **[Hitting GUARDS]** Trees, nitwits! Trees! Trees! Trees! As far as the eye can see.
	ALL GUARDS: Of course. Obvious really. Silly me. Etc
SOUND: 5 second Chainsaw	SHER: But – and here's the wonderfully wicked bit - a week from now and all these trees will be so much.... Sawdust! Now you see them...**[mimes chainsaw,** calling] Timber! Now you don't. So, pathetic pygmies, pack your bags and go. Sherwood is ripe for development. Houses, houses, everywhere and not a tree to be seen. Wave Sherwood Forest bye-bye.
	LADY: The clock's ticking, my little Lilliputians. We don't want a big old tree to fall and bash you on the bonce, now do we?
	SHER: [laughing, sings to the tune of 'Gonna Wash That Man Right Out of My Hair', exiting] 'We're gonna turn this forest into hard cash...."
	LADY: "We're gonna turn this forest into hard cash...."
	SHER: "We're gonna turn this forest into hard cash, and....[stops] There's not a single thing you can do to stop us! [SHER, LADY & GUARDS exit, singing.]
	[Pause]
	ALL DWARFS: [except ALGIE rush off] Snow White! Snow White!
LIGHTS: FADE 1-7	ALGIE: Oh, dear. Oh, dear. Oh, dear. [to audience] This doesn't look good, does it? [ALGIE exits after DWARFS] **Wait for me!**

Appendix IV - Rehearsal Schedule

FRI 4th JAN:
6.00 to 7.00 – pages 6 & 7: Snow White & Dwarfs
7.00 to 8.00 – pages 9-12: Robin & his Gang
8.00 to 9.00 – Lumberjacks
8.30 to 9.30 – pages 3-5: Sheriff, Lady & guards

TUES 8th JAN:
6.30 to 7.30 – pages 1-3: Dame & Market Traders
7.30 to 9.00 – pages 12-14: Three Little Pigs
8.00 to 9.00 – pages 12-14: (as above) & Wolf

FRI 11th JAN:
6.00 to 7.00 – pages 6 & 7: Snow White & Dwarfs
7.00 to 8.45 – pages 15 &16: Snow White & Robin
8.45 to 9.45 – pages 9-12: Robin & his Gang
9.15 to 9.45 - pages 17-18 (as above) & Sheriff

TUES 15th JAN:
6.30 to 7.15 - pages 1-3: Dame & Market traders
7.15 to 8.15 – pages 12-14, 18-19: Three Little Pigs & Wolf
8.15 to 9.00 - Lumberjacks & Wolf

FRI 18th JAN:
6.00 to 6.45 – pages 6 & 7: Snow White & Dwarfs
6.45 to 7.15 – pages 7 & 8: Dwarfs, Sheriff, Lady, Guards
7.15 to 9.00 – pages 9-12, 15-16, 17-18, 19-21: Snow White, Robin, Gang, + Sheriff

TUES 22nd JAN:
7.00 to 7.45 - pages 1- 3: Dame, Market Traders
7.45 to 8.30 – pages12-14, 18-19: Three Little Pigs, Wolf

FRI 25th JAN:
6.00 to 7.00 - All Dwarf Scenes: Snow White & Dwarfs
7.00 to 8.00 – pages 9-12, 15-16, 17-18, 19-21: Snow White, Robin, Gang, + Sheriff
8.00 to 8.30 – Dame, Lady – Food Scene
8.30 to 9.00 - Wolf & Lumberjacks (Song)

TUES 29th JAN:
6.30 - 7.00 – Wolf, Snow White
7.00 - 7.45 - pages 1-3: Dame, Market Traders
7.45 - 8.30 - Three Little Pigs (Song)

FRI 1st FEB:
6.00 to 7.00 – pages 14-15, 18, pages 7 & 8: Snow White, Dwarfs
7.00 to 7.20 – (as above) plus Robin, Gang
7.20 to 7.40 – page 7 & 8: Snow White, Dwarfs, Sheriff, Lady, Guards
7.40 onwards - page 23 to the end, including Chase: Sheriff, Lady, Guards, Lumberjacks, Snow White, Robin, Gang, Dwarfs [excluding youngest], Wolf, Three Little Pigs (This will take time to organise, so please be ready to be patient!)
8.40 to 9.30 - pages 21-23: Dame, Lady, Sheriff, Lady, Guards

TUES 5th FEB:
7.00 - 7.45 - pages 1-3: Dame, Market Traders
7.45 - 8.30 - Three Little Pigs Song/Scenes

FRI 8th FEB:
6.00 - 7.30 – All scenes with Robin, Snow White, Gang (+ Sheriff - c7.00)
7.30 - 8.00 – pages 4-5: Sheriff, Lady, Guards, Lumberjacks
8.00 - 8.20 – Wolf & Lumberjacks
8.20 - 9.00 – [Bits & Pieces – to be decided]

TUES 12th FEB:
7.00 - 7.45 - pages 1-3: Dame, Market Traders
7.45 - 8.30 - Three Little Pigs Song + Scenes with Wolf

FRI 15th FEB:
6.00 – 6.40 - pages 19 to 21: Snow White, Dwarfs, Robin, Gang, Dwarfs
6.40 - 7.30 - page 23 to the end: Dwarfs, Sheriff, Lady, Guards, Lumberjacks, Snow White, Robin, Gang, Wolf, Three Little Pigs
7.30 - 8.15 - pages 21 to 23 Banquet Scene: Lady, Dame, Sheriff, Lady, Guards
8.15 - 9.00 - pages 1-3: Dame, Market Traders

TUES 19th FEB:
7.00 - 7.45 - Three Little Pigs Song + Scenes with Wolf

FRI 22nd FEB:
6.00 - 6.30 – Snow White & Dwarfs
6.30 - 7.30: ACT 1, Scenes 1 + 2: Dame, Market Traders, Sheriff, Lady, Guards, Dwarfs, Snow White, Lumberjacks, Wolf
7.30 - 8.15 - ALL scenes with Robin, Snow White, Gang
8.15 - 9.00 – to be decided

FRI 1st MAR: FULL RUN of PART 1
7.00 onwards (pg1 to pg 14) – Dame, Market Traders, Wolf, Snow White, Dwarfs, Sheriff, Lady, Guards, Lumberjacks, Robin, Gang, Three Little Pigs

TUES 5th MAR - to be decided

FRI 8th MAR: FULL RUN of PART 2
7.00 onwards (page 14 onwards) – Dwarfs, Snow White, Sheriff, Lady, Guards, Lumberjacks, Snow White, Robin, Gang, Wolf, Three Little Pigs, Dame

TUES 12th MAR: to be decided

FRI 15th MAR: 7.00 onwards FULL RUNTHROUGH - EVERYONE

MON 18th MAR:- PLEASE KEEP FREE in case we need it.

TUES 19th MAR: 7.00 onwards TECHNICAL REHEARSAL - EVERYONE

FRI 22nd MAR: 7.00 onwards DRESS REHEARSAL – EVERYONE

FRI 23rd MAR: SHOWTIME!!!! At 2.30pm and at 7.30pm – EVERYONE!!!!!!!!

Appendix V - Pantos Performed

Here are the pantos we have performed from 1993 to 2013:

Ali Baba and the Forty Thieves - 1993
Mother Hubbard - 1995
The Grand Old Duchess of York - 1998
Aladdin and the Princesses - 2001
The Princess and the Dragon - 2003
Red Riding Hood - 2005
Dick Whittington - 2007
The Magic Cupboard - 2009
The Grand Old Duke of York - 2011
Robin Hood - 2013

Index

INDEX of main topics and themes:

Adlibs: 146-148

Asides: 51-53, 144-146

Audience, How to get one: 155-160

Audience, Talking to: 138-143

Audience Participation: 143-148

Auditions: 80

Availability: 25, 80

Bar: 178-179, 186, 191

Box Office: 157-160, 185-199

Car Parking: 176-177

Casting/Auditions: 78-80

Changing Rooms: 148-151, 185-199

Chases: 131-133

Choosing the Pantomime: 18-19, Appendix V

Community: 12-15, 19-25, 78-79, 204-212, Appendix I

Costumes: 82-86, 127-130, 149-151, 185-199, 203-204

Director: 100-103, 113-115, 131, 134, 152-154, 170, 172, 183-199

Dress Rehearsal: 148-154

Exits and Entrances: 92-94

Financing: 85-86

Front of House: 175-176, 183-199

Learning Lines: 110-113, 115-117

Lighting: 164-168, 183-199, Appendix III

Make-Up: 151-152

Performance(s): 183-199

Production Assistants: 118, 169, 170-172, 183-199

Production Mementoes: 179-182

Programme: 173-175

Prompter: 115

Props: 168-169, 200-202

Publicity and Promotion: 155-160, 180-182

Recruiting: 16, 19-25, 78-79

Refreshments: 177-178, 191

Rehearsals – Drawing up a Schedule: 96-99, 137-138, Appendix IV

Rehearsals – Managing: 99-133 ,134-136

Rehearsals – Getting a Performance: 103-107

Rehearsals – Motivating Children: 119-127

Rehearsals – Motivating Adults: 130-131

Rehearsals – Stagecraft: 107-109

Rehearsals – Pace: 115-116

Rehearsals – Volume: 117

Scenery and Set: 87-94, 200-202

Script –Writing/Adapting - guidelines: 27-33

Script – Naming characters: 31-33

Script – Rhyming or not: 34-39

Script – Writing for Baddies: 39-40

Script – Alliterating: 40-44

Script – Writing for Goodies: 44-47

Script – Writing Relationships: 47-74

Script – Dames: 48-51, 70-74

Script – Heroes and Heroines: 51-54

Script – Hero and his Gang: 54-59

Script – Villain and Villainess: 59-62
Script – Villains and their Cronies: 62-64
Script – Double Acts: 65-74
Script – Crowd Scenes: 74-76
Script – Songs and Music: 76-77
Script – Recycling Material: 78
Script – Providing Copies: 80-81
Sound and Special Effects: 161-164, 183 –199, Appendix III
Stage Levels: 91-92, Appendix II
Tickets: 157-158
Venue: 17-18, 155-156

PANTO: The MANUAL
© Village Voices 2015

Printed in Great Britain
by Amazon